ANYTHING FOR A HIT

ANYTHING FOR A HIT

An A&R Woman's Story of Surviving the Music Industry

DOROTHY CARVELLO

CHICAGO
REVIEW
PRESS

An A Cappella Book

Published by Chicago Review Press Incorporated
814 North Franklin Street
Chicago, Illinois 60610
978-0-912777-91-7

Library of Congress Cataloging-in-Publication Data
Names: Carvello, Dorothy, author.
Title: Anything for a hit : an A&R woman's story of surviving the music
  industry / Dorothy Carvello.
Description: Chicago, Illinois : Chicago Review Press, [2018]
Identifiers: LCCN 2018014941 (print) | LCCN 2018021036 (ebook) | ISBN
  9780912777924 (PDF edition) | ISBN 9780912777931 (EPUB edition) | ISBN
  9780912777948 (Kindle edition) | ISBN 9780912777917 (cloth edition)
Subjects: LCSH: Carvello, Dorothy. | Women sound recording executives and
  producers—United States—Biography. | Sound recording executives and
  producers—United States—Biography. | Sexual harassment. | LCGFT:
  Autobiographies.
Classification: LCC ML429.C23 (ebook) | LCC ML429.C23 A3 2018 (print) | DDC
  338.4/778092 [B] —dc23
LC record available at https://lccn.loc.gov/2018014941

Typesetting: Nord Compo

Printed in the United States of America
5 4 3 2 1

For Thomas

"The music business is a cruel and shallow money trench, a long plastic hallway where thieves and pimps run free, and good men die like dogs. There's also a negative side."

—Hunter S. Thompson

CONTENTS

I would like to thank my team for making this book possible:
David Vigliano
Thomas Flannery Jr.
Travis Atria
Yuval Taylor
Amanda Kusek

And thank you to:
Michele Anthony, Gary Baker, Jerry Blair, Jamie Brenner, Allen Brown, Bob Buziak, Joey Carvello, Rich Christina, Tim Collins, John Connolly, Joey DeMaio, Frank DiGiacomo, Sam Evans, Wendy Flom, Jennifer Goodman, Randy Goodman, Jerry Greenberg, Don Ienner, Richard Johnson, Craig Kallman, Isabel Kallman, John David Kalodner, Joel Katz, David Korzenik, Richard Landis, Bill Liebowitz, Leila Logan, John Luongo, Nick Maria, Linda Moran, Mike Moran, Chris Murphy, Deborah Radel, Eric Rayman, Bruce Roberts, Janice Roeg, Dave "Snake" Sabo, Richie Sambora, Derek Shulman, Raymond Sicignano, Martha Troup, Diane Warren, Fred Wistow, and Larry Yasgar.

THE MEN (THEN)

Ahmet Ertegun—Founder and Chairman of Atlantic Records
Doug Morris—President of Atlantic Records
Jason Flom—A&R Executive, Atlantic Records
Joey Carvello—Director of Promotion at WTG
Craig Kallman—President and Owner of Big Beat Records
Irving Azoff—Chairman of MCA Music Entertainment Group
Charlie Minor—Executive Vice President of Promotion, A&M Records
Joe Galante—President of RCA's Nashville Division
Randy Goodman—Senior Vice President of Marketing, RCA Records Nashville
Frank DiLeo—Manager, Michael Jackson
Bob Buziak—President of RCA Records
Donnie Ienner—President of Columbia Records
Tommy Mottola—Chairman and CEO of Sony U.S.

FAST FORWARD

New York City, 2006: My phone rings. It's Ahmet Ertegun, founder of Atlantic Records.

"Come visit me," he says. "I'm lonely."

Ahmet is perhaps the most revered man in the music business. If the word "legend" has any meaning, Ahmet is a legend. He started his career in 1947 with an interest in jazz, blues, and R&B. He signed acts such as Professor Longhair and Big Joe Turner, and he wrote several blues classics, such as "Sweet Sixteen" and "Chains of Love." In the 1950s, he signed a young Ray Charles and wrote "Mess Around," Charles's first hit on Atlantic. In the 1960s, he made a deal with Stax Records to distribute genre-defining albums by Otis Redding, Wilson Pickett, and Solomon Burke, and he snatched Aretha Franklin from Columbia Records and took her back to her gospel roots, resulting in landmark albums such as *I Never Loved a Man the Way I Love You* and *Lady Soul*. In the late 1960s, he turned his gaze to rock music. He signed Crosby, Stills & Nash and convinced them to add Neil Young; he signed Eric Clapton, Yes, and Led Zeppelin; Zeppelin recorded four diamond records for Atlantic (awarded for ten million sales or more, this designation has been given to only ninety records in history). In the early 1970s, he made a label deal with the Rolling Stones, and they rewarded him with *Exile on Main St.*

He is more than just a record executive. He is a visionary. He created the Rock & Roll Hall of Fame, and his acts largely populate it. He

1

is a statesman, fostering ties between America and his native Turkey. His friends include world leaders in art, finance, and politics—people like Henry Kissinger and Oscar de la Renta. He has earned a Grammy Trustees Award for lifetime achievements, an honorary doctorate from Berklee College of Music, and a Living Legend award from the Library of Congress. None of that keeps him company, though.

He has a wife, Mica, but she was always more of a front than a spouse—a respectable veneer to hide the depravity within. His infidelity has long been an open secret. He even took a date to his own wedding. He also has an ex-wife, but he never speaks of her. I did see a picture of her once. Ahmet's longtime assistant Noreen Woods was busy one afternoon cataloging his files when she found a photograph of the woman and slid it across my desk.

"Look," she said. The woman looked like Ulla from *The Producers*—a total blonde bombshell.

"Whatever happened to her?" I asked.

"I don't know," Noreen said. "But I met her. I was with Ahmet at the Plaza Athénée in Paris when this beautiful blonde came up and started talking to him. I realized it was his ex-wife. When they finished talking she gave him a hug and a kiss—what you'd expect from an amicable ex-relationship."

"I can't believe you met her," I interrupted.

"Wait, this is the best part," Noreen continued. "When she walked away, Ahmet said to me, 'Who was that?'"

Classic Ahmet.

That's why he's alone. It's Classic Ahmet's fault. Classic Ahmet was the guy who played with himself under his desk while dictating letters to his secretary. Classic Ahmet was the guy whose nightly routine included four lines of cocaine. Classic Ahmet was the guy who couldn't be bothered to remember people's names—he called Jann Wenner, cofounder and publisher of *Rolling Stone*, "That Faggot," not to be confused with Paul Cooper, general manager of Atlantic's West Coast office, who was "That Fucking Faggot in L.A."

Classic Ahmet had power and influence, which kept people close to him even while he abused them. Now his power and influence have waned, and those people have nothing to gain by coming to visit an old man. And so, he's lonely.

I feel the need to be there for him. When I enter his double townhouse in Manhattan, I see the man I still revere despite everything, the man who gave me my first job in the music business and remained a trusted adviser during my two decades working for Atlantic and other major labels. He's also the man who verbally, physically, and sexually mistreated me.

He's worse for wear, blind in one eye and hobbling on two fake hips, yet he's still the very picture of posh cosmopolitan life. He wears custom pajamas from Savile Row, velvet slippers, and a silk robe with an ascot. His apartment is littered with the works of masters like it's the Metropolitan Museum of Art. He leans on his cane and hobbles past his Picasso, past his Degas, past his Pollock, and past his Hockney, to greet me.

"Show me your pussy," he says. "For old time's sake."

He's never seen my pussy. That's just more Classic Ahmet.

I sit down and we reminisce. He's bitter—bitter about selling Atlantic to Warner CEO Steve Ross for $17.5 million in 1967, when he should have gotten more; bitter that his company is now privately owned; bitter that his perks have been cut back; bitter that he lost his grip on the awesome power he wielded for half a century.

It's hard to feel bad for him. His sense of entitlement is enormous. He was raised in a well-heeled Turkish family. His father, Mehmet Ertegun, served as legal counsel to Kemal Ataturk, the founder of modern Turkey. Mehmet became the Turkish ambassador to the United States and counted President Franklin D. Roosevelt as a friend. When Mehmet died, Roosevelt arranged to have his body sent back to Turkey on the USS *Missouri*.

Ahmet is also a triple-digit millionaire. When Warner merged with Time Inc. in 1989, Steve Ross gave Ahmet inside information (highly illegal), and Ahmet made a killing (also illegal). The two men shared an enemy—David Geffen—and, in a move Ahmet should have appreciated, Ross didn't give Geffen the inside info. In retaliation, Geffen pulled out of his deal with Warner and sold his company to MCA.

These men were petty, and Ahmet is as petty as they come. It doesn't matter that Ross helped make him rich. He can't see beyond his disdain. He calls Ross "the Undertaker," a dig at Ross's lowly beginning as a funeral-home director. As far as Ahmet is concerned, Ross is a peasant. Ahmet considers most people peasants. It's his favorite insult. I can't count the times he hurled it at me after I fucked up.

I don't mention any of this, of course. And, truth be told, as we chat in his townhouse, I do feel bad for him. He reminds me of the old Rolling Stones song "Sympathy for the Devil": *Please allow me to introduce myself / I'm a man of wealth and taste.* That's Ahmet. Somehow, I've always felt sympathy for him.

Maybe that's why he trusts me enough to air his most intimate regrets. He complains he didn't get what he wanted out of life. He blames it on his mother—she loved his brother Nesuhi more than she loved him. He blames it on his wife—all those years spent with Mica, when Janice (his mistress) was the one he really wanted.

Why is it always the woman who gets blamed? I think, but I don't say anything. My mind flashes back to our first meeting. I was a nervous twenty-four-year-old girl, fresh out of college, and desperate for a job in the music business, sitting across from Ahmet at his enormous desk in his palatial office. The difference between us couldn't have been more pronounced.

Sitting across from him now in his townhouse, that old gulf between us evaporates. I realize how similar we are. I never found true love either. My career didn't go how I hoped it would. He has many millions of dollars more than me, but he's not better off than me, not when it comes to what truly matters. In a way, he's teaching me one last lesson: when you get to the end of your life and wonder what it was all for, no amount of success, or fame, or money, or power, or pussy can replace love, or friendship, or happiness.

As Ahmet continues to pity himself, a heat rises within me. I want him to understand what I went through, to think of me just once after all these years. Finally, I say something: "What about me? I didn't get what I wanted either. Why was I held back from my dreams?"

He looks at me with his one good eye. "What did you expect?" he says. "You're a woman."

PART I

ATLANTIC RECORDS

1

REWIND

I WAS BORN IN BROOKLYN in 1962 to a working-class Italian American family. My mother was an unfulfilled housewife; my father was a gambling addict. She worshipped the ground he walked on; he wouldn't give her the time of day if he worked in a clock factory. You could have torn us from a Scorsese film—one of those period pieces on the Italian immigrant experience—except no one in my family had an association with the Mafia. Yet.

My father and I had no real relationship. He was a narcissist, and our lives revolved around his gambling addiction, without any thought for what it did to us. The best I can say is he never hit us—his father beat him as a child, and he didn't believe in administering discipline that way. He also didn't believe in administering anything. He was absent. He worked a civil service job and did real estate deals on the side, but as soon as the money came in, he'd gamble it away. He took night shifts as a waiter to pay his debts. On weekends, he'd make himself scarce.

My mother didn't know how much money my father made. If he gave her five dollars for the week, we had to find a way to live on it. I remember going two straight years as a child without new shoes. I assumed we were poor, and so did my mother. I didn't learn until later that we were actually middle class, or at least we would have been had my father not gambled our money away. I revered my mother. If this life was good enough for her, what right did I have to expect better?

I have two older brothers, but when it came to chores and housework, the responsibilities all fell on me. At the tender age of six, I learned my duties: "Bebe," my mother said (Bebe was my nickname; Ahmet was the first person in my life to call me Dorothy), "you have to clear the table and wash the dishes every night."

"Why?" I said. "They eat too, but they don't have to clean up."

"We're not talking about them."

"Why aren't we talking about them? What's the difference?"

She grabbed my arm and pulled me to the sink. "Do the dishes," she said.

"I can't reach the sink."

She got her wooden spoon, gave me a couple of whacks on the ass, and set up a bench. Every night, while my brothers lived wild and free, I had to set and clear the table and wash dishes like I was in the army. That's when I first discovered the difference between boys and girls.

I felt rejected at birth just by being female. It wasn't something to be cherished or honored. It was a burden to bear. The message was: men live for themselves; women live for men. I saw this message repeated everywhere, from my brothers, to my parents, to my aunts, who pretended to be modern but were just as backward as the rest of them.

I also have a younger sister. My parents spoiled her in comparison to the rest of us—they had more money by the time she came. When she turned six years old, I didn't want to do the dishes anymore. I asked my mother if my sister could start doing the dishes, and my mother said, "No, she has to develop at her own rate." There was another message: if you have to be a woman, at least don't be the oldest one.

My mother devoted her life to taking care of others, and she trained me to do the same. It was like a script I had to follow. The playbill of life listed my role as girl who follows men around with a broom and a mop. It seemed like a bum deal, but every time I tried to wrestle my way out of it, someone came along waving the script in my face. *Don't get any bright ideas*, they'd say. *Know your role.*

Life under these conditions left no room for fantasy. "Look at where you come from," my mother would say, tethering me to reality. "Look at how you look, how you speak. This is the best you can hope for." To even acknowledge my needs and desires felt selfish and wrong.

Sometimes I'd see a crack in my mother's facade, a glimpse into her inner life with all its stunted desires and unused talents. In those rare glimpses, I sensed a mother's tenderness. One particular moment stands out. I was ten years old, it was the Saturday before Christmas, and she took me to lunch at Abraham & Straus, a high-end department store in Brooklyn. Walking past the toy department, I mooned over a stuffed Siamese cat in the display window. It must have cost about eight dollars—serious money back then—but I begged for it. My mother said, "I know you want it, but Christmas is coming and we can't afford it." I upped the ante, threatening to make a scene the way children do. She relented. God only knows what she must have sacrificed to buy that stuffed cat, but I cherished it. I still have it in my bedroom today.

Despite my mother's occasional shows of support, I felt no encouragement from the rest of my family. No one jerks you off in an Italian household. If I expressed any determination, any dreams or ambitions, I got smacked down. "You're too stupid," they'd say.

Life outside the house wasn't much better. One year my uncle took us to see Santa Claus in the old *Daily News* building on Forty-Second Street. Santa Claus asked what I wanted for Christmas. I said an Easy-Bake Oven. I knew I wasn't getting the oven. I just wanted to dream. He said, "I can't give that to you because you might burn yourself." *Motherfucker*, I thought. *Even Santa Claus won't jerk me off.*

Once or twice, my mother tried to warn me away from her life. She told me the most important job in life is being a mother, but she cautioned, "Don't do it unless you're prepared to give one hundred percent." She told me I could do better and I believed her.

At the same time, my own desires were crushed under insurmountable guilt. I learned to feel the guilt at home and had it drilled into my skull at Catholic school. Those Irish Catholic nuns didn't fuck around. They believed in an angry God and built their world around repression and retribution. These women never had a normal, healthy human impulse they didn't despise.

As an Italian girl in an Irish school, I was treated like low-rent riffraff. I didn't fit in with my classmates. I disliked my last name—Sicignano. It was so long and no one could pronounce it. It was massacred at every Communion and graduation. It was just one more thing that set me apart from my classmates. Even my bread was different. When I brought a sandwich for lunch, I had Italian bread while my classmates all had Wonder Bread. I'd tell my mother, "I want a sandwich like everyone else has." What could she do? We were Italian.

I always had my face pressed against the glass looking at what other people had. I never lived the life of a happy, carefree kid. I was, however, independent. I put myself to bed at eight thirty every night, unprompted. We wore school uniforms, and I had only one shirt, so every night I had to wash it, hang it on the clothesline, take it in, and iron it. I began doing this in the second grade. I never asked my mother for help.

Even my independence came off wrong, though. The kids on my block called me "Bossy Bebe," a name that filled me with shame. Everyone told me I had a big mouth and a stubborn mind. Again, the message came through loud and clear: girls aren't leaders. To have a backbone, or even an opinion, was not acceptable. I'll never forget the advice I got from Sister Rose Ellen in the sixth grade. She took me aside and said, "You have leadership qualities. Men are going to try to break you."

I only felt free while listening to music. One of my first memories is hearing a song called "Take a Letter Maria" on the radio. While the music played, anything seemed possible. One of my brothers also collected records, and I'd eavesdrop on him spinning the latest from the Beatles, the Rolling Stones, and Led Zeppelin. I'll also never forget the time I saw John Lennon in Manhattan. He looked right at me and passed an electric current through me that I can still feel today.

I grew up in the heyday of classic rock, when listening to the right bands made you cool. I liked the sense of belonging to the in-crowd, but I also took great interest in the way these bands turned their fantasies into reality. It fascinated me that someone could release an eight-minute-long song like "Stairway to Heaven" or "Hey Jude" and make every second of it so enthralling that radio stations had no choice but to spin it. *What freedom, to bend the world around your will.*

As a child, I dabbled in music. I began classical piano lessons in the second grade and continued for five years. My mother could barely afford the two dollars a lesson, but she insisted that I keep taking them. It was another sacrifice she made, another glimpse into that other world. I loved the piano, and I might have developed a knack for it, but my teacher was one of those old-fashioned nuns who seemed to revel in killing joy. She'd sit next to me on the piano bench, dressed head to toe in her habit, and slam my fingers on the keyboard if I missed a note. Those kinds of methods never worked on me. Hitting, yelling, and reprimanding made me defiant. I'd do the opposite of what I was told to do. That's how it went in my career, too. If I had the right teacher, I excelled. If not, I rebelled.

In grade school, I found a different kind of freedom in running track. I was always fast, and running appealed to me. I suppose it makes sense—symbolically, at least, I was running away from my life. But life always catches up. At birth, I had a benign tumor in my knee, and when I turned twelve, it began pressing against the bone and causing intense pain. I had a biopsy at age twelve and a surgery at age sixteen to remove the tumor (I had to have a second operation when I was twenty-one).

After that first surgery, I spent three weeks in a hospital bed with nothing to do but contemplate my direction in life. *This can't be me, an invalid trapped in a world with no prospects.* As I hobbled around on crutches for the next several months, I felt a fire burning within me. I had to get the fuck out of Brooklyn. I had to be better than my family. With the arrogance of a teenager, I saw them as slobs who couldn't get out of their own way; only later did I realize what a burden it must have been for my parents to take the train to a Manhattan hospital and pay medical expenses they couldn't afford. Regardless, it was a turning point in my life. I had to escape.

Leave it to my mother to plot my escape. I never had any plan of going to college—it wasn't done in my family—but after graduating high school, I came home to find an acceptance letter from Marymount Manhattan College. My mother had filled out the application and sent it without telling me. In her youth, she was desperate to attend college herself but had to drop out because she couldn't afford it. Now, she was making sure I had the chance. It was another subtle kindness, another glimpse behind the veil.

During college, I lived at home and commuted to school, where I majored in political science. It was a women's college staffed mostly by nuns, giving me a false confidence in what women could achieve in the workplace. I found the classes difficult, but I got through them. In my junior and senior year, I even excelled.

After college, I decided to join the FBI. Many people in my family worked in civil service, and the advantages of these jobs had been impressed on me since birth. It was steady work with a pension. Plus, I believed in truth, justice, and the American way. I wanted to lock up scumbags. Also, the prospect of joining an organization dedicated to justice seemed like a nice tribute to Sister Rose Ellen. I filled out the application and quickly received a response. They accepted me, but first I had to prove I had held the same job for twenty-four months.

OK, where could I work for two years?

2

THE JOKER

IT WAS MID-1985 AND I needed a job. I felt anxious to get into Quantico, but at the rate I was going, it seemed permanently out of reach. I had found temporary work at *Redbook* magazine, but despite the glitz and glamour that came with my title—temp receptionist—I needed more.

During the dreary morning subway commute, I daydreamed that I was a rich and powerful music executive. I had always revered musicians—to this day, I am in awe of anyone who can write a song. The music business seemed like it would give me everything I wanted but couldn't get: status, power, money, and the forbidden thrills of sex and rock 'n' roll (drugs didn't interest me). It was just an idle fantasy. I had no qualifications and no connections to get my foot in the door. But life is strange, and my luck was about to change thanks to a tiny island off the coast of Syria.

Glancing at the *New York Daily News* on the subway one morning, I noticed an article describing an escalating conflict in the island nation of Cyprus, which seethed under its second decade of Turkish occupation. The conflict had caught the attention of the head of the US Armed Services Committee, Congressman Stephen Solarz, whose mother happened to be a family friend. Solarz planned to appropriate money for finding a solution in Cyprus, and one of his fundraisers, the article noted, was a Turk named Ahmet Ertegun. He happened to be the founder of Atlantic Records.

Foot, meet door.

Unfortunately, my connection to Solarz's mother proved weaker than I thought, and I couldn't ask her for a favor, but my head is hard as a rock when I want something. I also had a friend, Peter Abbate, who had worked for Solarz and was running for the New York State Assembly. Peter said if I worked on his campaign he would have Solarz's chief of staff set up an appointment with Ahmet. Six months of stuffing envelopes and hanging signs later, I called in my favor with Peter. Nothing happened. I waited and waited, clicking my heels to no avail.

In the spring of 1986, I finally got my interview. I entered Rockefeller Plaza, took the elevator to the second floor, and entered the offices of the famed Atlantic Records. The place looked like shit. Atlantic, I would learn, was notorious for cheapness. Clumps of shabby, mismatched furniture dotted the waiting room. The offices all had a miser's touch. Even Doug Morris, president of the company, had an office fit for a low-level peon. The only nice office in Atlantic's headquarters—the only room with matching furniture, even—was Ahmet's. It was a sign of his power, as was Atlantic's position on the second floor, where the views ranged from terrible to nonexistent. Ahmet was terrified of fire and wanted a quick escape if the building burned down, so he chose the second floor and everyone had to deal with it. That was the thing about Ahmet: he never heard the word no.

You had to give Ahmet credit, though—he'd earned it. Gold records (awarded for five hundred thousand sales) lined the Atlantic hallways like wallpaper, a sight fit to impress a jaded industry veteran, never mind a girl from Brooklyn. As I walked down the hall, I recognized albums I'd loved as a kid, including "Take a Letter Maria," which Ahmet had produced.

His office was the size of a two-bedroom Manhattan apartment. He sat dwarfed behind a desk so large it could have doubled as a ping-pong table. He didn't make a great first impression—he was a short, bald, old man with round glasses, a goatee, and a yellow-toothed grin—but taking a seat opposite him emphasized the gulf that separated my world from his. I lusted for that world, yearned to be considered worthy of it, even if only for a few years before starting at the FBI. This was my one shot at freedom before I inevitably took on my mother's life.

Ahmet began the interview. It came as a slight relief that he didn't have a copy of my résumé in front of him, considering it was complete bullshit.

"So you just graduated?" he asked.

"Yes—well, a year ago."

"What school?"

"Marymount."

I was proud of my degree. Most people in my family didn't even go to college. For all it meant to Ahmet, though, I might as well have named a clown college. Virtually everyone on his level was an Ivy League grad. This was my second inkling that Ahmet existed in a higher stratum than anyone I knew.

"What were you thinking of doing in music?" he asked.

"Publicity," I said. I didn't even know what publicity meant in the record industry, but I liked parties.

"You're a woman; you have to start at the bottom," he said. I wasn't sure what he was getting at. Obviously I didn't expect to be appointed head of the Publicity Department.

"I guess I'm looking for an assistant publicist position," I said, demoting myself before the first interview had even ended. Granted, I wasn't qualified for anything other than an entry-level position. Maybe I wasn't even qualified for that—I couldn't type or take dictation—but in later years, I'd see many incompetent men get promotions they hadn't earned to jobs they weren't qualified for. Yet even after I had learned the business and proven myself, I still didn't feel right asking for what I was worth.

Women today deal with the same issue, but we have ways of talking about it. For instance, this particular problem—that women often don't feel comfortable asking for what they're worth—is called the "ask gap." People study it, compile charts and figures based on it, and look for ways to combat it. Back then, though, there were no studies, there were no terms like "ask gap," and there were precious few successful women to lead the fight.

Perhaps Ahmet sensed my diffidence. He had a knack for that sort of thing. He said four words—"There aren't any jobs"—and the interview was over. He delivered this blow so matter-of-factly I almost didn't understand him. I was sure they would find something for me: it was a political favor, I had a college degree, and I'd take a job rearranging the supply closet if I had to. How could he not want to hire me?

I shook his hand and exited his office, feeling crushed. I had come in expecting a favor from the king, and I left feeling like an empty-handed peasant. As I walked to the elevator, Ahmet's assistant, Jenny, stopped me. She was a pretty African American woman, heavyset with a beautiful face and the type of skin that never needed makeup.

"How'd it go?" she asked.

"Not good."

"Don't sweat it," she said with a shrug that told me she could take her job or leave it.

"You're not happy here?" I asked.

"It pays the bills."

"I'm Dorothy, by the way."

"Jenny."

As I chatted with Jenny, I realized that she knew Ahmet's calendar better than he did. She could control who was let in and who got cut off. I had just intuited my first lesson in business: the way into the castle is through the caretaker, not the king.

"We should have lunch sometime," I said to Jenny. "You can scare me off the music business and make me feel better about not having a job."

"As long as you're buying," she said. "I don't have an expense account."

"Right," I said.

Note to self: find out what an expense account is.

———————

A few weeks later, I met Jenny outside Atlantic's offices, and we went to a coffee shop on Fifty-Second Street. She talked and I listened. Jenny made it clear that Ahmet didn't reward his employees with perks. "The money's shit," she said, but she said it with a mischievous smile that reminded me of myself. I could tell she knew the feeling of being undervalued. She knew what it meant to work hard with no hope of promotion. She worked for a major record company, and she was no better off than a fresh college graduate temping at a magazine. I shuddered with a futile sense of sadness. *Was this the best a woman could hope for?* Still, my determination remained unbroken.

My older brother had just opened a nightclub in Tribeca, and I had come prepared to dangle the club like a carrot in front of Jenny's underpaid eyes. You know the old saying "I'll scratch your back if you scratch mine"? Well, I knew just where Jenny itched.

I told her about the club and said, "Would you be interested in making some money? We need to get a crowd."

"Do you want Ahmet's crowd or a younger crowd?" she said.

Ahmet, I learned, had many crowds. He had three Rolodexes, each for a different social set. The first Rolodex was for close friends, important socialites, trustworthy drug dealers, and girls. The second Rolodex was for music executives, media moguls, and band managers. The third was for the moderately important, the semipowerful, and the quasi-estranged. Jenny sounded interested in helping with the club and said she'd think it over. As promised, I picked up the tab, and I left thinking she was too smart and talented to be someone's assistant. I sensed she felt stuck and decided I wasn't going to fall into the same trap.

Meanwhile, I still needed a job. My brother gave me a position as a cashier at his club, but it wasn't an ideal situation for a girl looking to work for the Feds. He had gotten the money to start the club from a mobster named Robert DiBernardo—DB for short. DB was a capo in the Gambino crime family, a partner of notorious hit man Sammy "the Bull" Gravano. These were not men to fuck with. A few months later, Gravano would help orchestrate DB's murder—one of nineteen murders he participated in.

At the time, DB and Gravano ran a pornography distribution company called Starr Productions, and they leased a warehouse on Lafayette Street. My brother took me there once, and I met Morty, the warehouse manager, who scurried around whipping out dildos, vibrators, and bottles of Spanish Fly, laughing at my horrified reactions. He told me the recipe for Spanish Fly was just plain water. Then he disappeared somewhere in the back of the warehouse and came lurching out of the shadows dressed head to toe in a latex S&M jumpsuit, complete with hooded mask. He looked like the Gimp from *Pulp Fiction.*

"Isn't this sick shit?" he said, peeling off the mask.

It was sick, at least by the moral standards of a nice Catholic girl. I just hoped Jenny could save me with a job at Atlantic before it was too late. What sweet innocence, to think the music business and the Mob were two separate entities.

Jenny agreed to help at the club, and she came through immediately, bringing in Bruce Carbone from Atlantic's Dance Department to hire DJs. She also showed a knack for promotion, and as I hoped, my brother offered to hire her as a consultant in return for a few thousand dollars. She did her part, but my brother wouldn't pay on time, causing me great embarrassment. As at any Mob-affiliated joint, however, much of the business was done in cash. I didn't think my brother would notice, so I took the money from the till and paid Jenny what she had earned. A few weeks later, out of the blue, I received a call inviting me to another interview with Ahmet.

Scratch, scratch.

———————

At that exact moment, my mother was diagnosed with cancer and underwent a serious surgery. I spent the weeks leading up to my second interview caring for her. For the first time in months, I had completely stopped thinking about my career. It was the necessary and right thing to do, but it took a toll. I showed up for my second interview with Ahmet sweating, feeling more nervous than the first time.

Ahmet, on the other hand, seemed more focused, making eye contact and glancing at a piece of paper on his desk. *Could that possibly be my résumé?*

"I have a job for you," Ahmet said. "But you're going to hate it."

"What's the position?"

"My secretary."

When Jenny had called me to set up the meeting, she seemed tight-lipped. Now I knew why. I was interviewing for a position even lower than hers.

"I'll take it," I said.

I was desperate. Ahmet asked if I knew how to type and take dictation, and I lied. I wasn't going to lose the gig over a silly little thing like a lack of qualifications. Besides, I had two weeks until the job started. I frantically signed up for a typing class and went to Coliseum Books on Fifty-Seventh Street for a book on shorthand. *If he fires me, he fires me.*

I started work on Monday, April 6, 1987, nine days before my twenty-fifth birthday. I got an office in the executive wing, near Atlantic president Doug Morris, vice chairman and CFO Sheldon Vogel, and of course, Ahmet. My official title was secretary to the chairman, or as Ahmet said it in his frog-croak voice, "sec-a-tary."

My office was in the middle of the hallway leading to the executive wing, making me an easy target. One executive walked past my office every day and said, "Blow me." I hadn't even met him. I was also across the hall from the head of A&R, Tunc Erim, the most vulgar, disgusting man of the bunch. He called everyone a cocksucker or a cunt, and he grabbed my ass constantly. I hated it.

These men were sending me a message: *Don't get comfortable here; you aren't important.* I got that message every day from nearly every man who worked at Atlantic. In large and small ways, they tried to chip away at my confidence and strip away my power.

Most of the men were too stupid to deliver that message with anything approaching finesse. Their attempts to degrade me were cartoonish—pinching my ass, bragging about their dicks, telling me to blow them. That's what made Doug Morris so powerful—and so dangerous. He was a master manipulator. He could ruin your life and you'd want to thank him for it. His favorite line after finishing a negotiation (often fucking someone out of serious money) was, "Did I act honorably?"

My first impression of Doug was exactly the opposite of the man I came to know, but it remains to this day. I found him extremely charming. I didn't learn the other side until I began to watch him behind the scenes. He had a gift for exploiting people's weaknesses. He mocked my Brooklyn accent, partly out of New York classism, and partly to fuck with my head. I never heard him make comments about other executives from London, Boston, or the South. I didn't understand why he made fun of me—where was my accent supposed to be from? I was born in

Brooklyn. Plus, Doug had a Long Island accent—he said "cawfee" instead of "coffee," "Lawng Island" instead of "Long Island"—and he spoke in a monotone voice like Anthony Hopkins in *Silence of the Lambs*. No one made fun of him. It put me on my back foot and made me defensive, which gave Doug the advantage, and yet he'd do it in such a way that I still liked him and needed his acceptance.

Like Ahmet, Doug led a charmed life. He had a driver take him to and from work every day. He cherished his Ivy League education and moved in an elite crowd. He was brilliant: Doug kept the whole business in his head. His file cabinets were empty except for a change of clothes and shoes. His days were spent taking and making phone calls, setting radio promotion priorities, signing acts, and taking meetings with artists, managers, producers, and staff, and he did it all off the cuff.

Doug liked people—that was the main difference between him and Ahmet. As much as he'd exploit our weaknesses, he could also manipulate our strengths to do what he needed to get done. That is a great gift of leadership, and that's why he's still around. Ahmet didn't have that gift. It seemed he only liked people who were on his level, people like "Dougie" (Ahmet was the only person allowed to call Doug that). For everyone else, Ahmet would call you an idiot as soon as look at you. His directions usually went something like: "Get me that moron on the phone."

The third big man on campus, Sheldon Vogel, was a misanthrope like Ahmet. He served as Atlantic's accountant and Ahmet's personal financial manager (on Atlantic's dime). He kept a ticker tape of the New York Stock Exchange in his office. That's how into money he was. Sheldon was a financial genius. He made Ahmet rich. He had a higher title than Doug Morris, but he repelled people. He was like cat shit, this guy. Nobody wanted to deal with him. He acted like we were all fucking idiots and buffoons, and he let us know it on a regular basis.

Still, I loved the job. I knew the nuns wouldn't have approved of anything that went on at Atlantic, and yet, I didn't care. Nothing about life up to that point had been fun. The nuns weren't fun. Catholic guilt wasn't fun. The FBI wasn't fun. My mother's cancer wasn't fun.

Atlantic was *fun*.

That week, I got my first big task: find Ahmet and get his signature on some financial papers. It was after hours, and he had already left the office, but I tracked him down at the Atlantic recording studio on Sixtieth Street and Broadway. He was producing an album for a commercial jingle singer turned Atlantic recording artist named Rachele Cappelli, who wasn't in the studio that night. When I arrived, I found Ahmet in the control room, pants and underwear down to the floor, getting a blow job.

He saw the papers in my hand and gave me a look I would come to know well. It said, "Are you in?" I held his gaze, feeling the pressure. *How badly do I want to roll with Ahmet? What would I do to enter his world?* I knew if I went along with this, there was no turning back. I walked to him calmly and handed him the papers. He signed them, mid–blow job, without a word.

So long, Quantico.

3

WE'RE NOT IN KANSAS ANYMORE

THE BATTLE FOR MY SOUL had begun. There was no honeymoon. I was plunged headfirst into what I can only describe as a circus mixed with an orgy. If personnel had actually enforced the rules, everyone in the building would have been fired by lunch.

My day started at 9:00 AM, but Ahmet didn't roll into the office until 3:00 PM. No one outside of Atlantic knew of his unusual schedule because I switched all calls to an extension at his house until he arrived. From nine until noon, when Doug's assistant arrived, I answered Doug's phone, ordered two coffees for him the way he liked it—milk and sugar—and did his general bidding, including running interference with his daily list of female callers.

Doug had many women who called him every day. People in the industry called them Doug's Dolls. The list included Reen Nalli, Laurie Weintraub, Lisa Hartman, Marilyn Martin, Allanah Myles (she danced on Tunc's desk for him), Diane Gibson (Atlantic star Debbie Gibson's mother), and Gloria Loring (Robin Thicke's mother). Many of these women got recording contracts from Doug.

The most important of Doug's Dolls was Atlantic recording artist Laura Branigan. Ahmet discovered Laura, and Ahmet told me that he and Laura had had an affair. I don't know if it was true, but it was the kind of thing these guys would do—exchange a record deal for sex, then toss the girl to someone else. Doug paid extra attention to Laura's career, finding songs like "Gloria" that she turned into hits, and ordering Peter Koepke, his A&R assistant, to scour Europe for other hit songs that Laura could cover. Doug seemed quite enamored with her. He never seemed happier than when he was with her or speaking about her. One day, after a meeting with Laura, he came out of his office and stood in the executive hallway; in front of the other assistants, he proclaimed that Laura was the love of his life. Of course, he was married at the time.

Doug gave me special instructions on how to answer the phone when she called. Every morning, he'd be with the senior vice president of promotion, Vince Faraci. When the phone rang and I heard, "It's Laura," I put her on hold, called Vince's extension, and asked for Doug. I told Doug—and only Doug—that Laura was on the phone. Then I watched Doug do what I called the hundred-yard dash, running from Vince's office all the way down the hall back to his office to answer the phone.

Despite the fact that he had so many women in his life, I sensed a deep loneliness in Doug. Sometimes in the morning, as I answered Ahmet's phones, Doug sat in my tiny office and made calls from my chair. It seemed like he just didn't want to be alone.

Ahmet's late arrival was due to his idiosyncrasies, not laziness. Despite his notorious penchant for partying until the wee hours, he didn't sleep late. Quite the opposite: I would barely have my coat off every morning when he'd call with the same three questions: "Where was I last night? What day is it? What time is it?"

The first two questions I understood. Ahmet lived hard. His nightly routine was fourteen vodka tonics, four lines of coke, and two joints. This usually came after smoking several joints in the Atlantic bathroom and having a few drinks in his office during the day. I marveled at his constitution. When he'd get fucked up, he'd leave credit cards all over town, and since I typed his nightly itinerary, he often needed my help to retrieve his personal effects the next day. But the third question—what time is it—I could never understand. He had a clock the size of Big Ben in his bedroom.

He occasionally invited me out on his nightly escapades. We weren't friendly yet; it was a function of my job. On those nights Ahmet put me in charge of his nightly cash—he'd spread his thumb and forefinger to show me the size of the stack he wanted, and I'd get it from the Atlantic accountant. It usually came to around $2,000, plus bribe money in case he got into trouble. He almost always got into trouble.

Everything was about sex at Atlantic. Discussing sex and having sex took up a large part of the day, and there was always time for pleasure on Ahmet's watch. There was a term for sex that we all used—"slapping it," or "slappage" for short. These words were hilarious coming from Ahmet's Turkish mouth. Few people saw this side of him.

I learned to be careful entering any office, because some executives watched pornography behind closed doors. They also walked around with pornographic magazines hidden in manila envelopes, and they'd read them during meetings. Is it any wonder these guys were sexual animals in the workplace? Watching porn all day got them hyped up and ready to go. This behavior created a culture of toxic masculinity.

The promotion department was the worst. Once I walked in on two promotion executives watching a Japanese porn movie while one of Atlantic's biggest stars sat with them eating Chinese food. Let's just say I felt it in the air. Another promotion executive decorated his office with dildos, S&M harnesses and ball gags, masks, lube, and a cat o' nine tails whip. It looked like the Pink Pussycat Boutique. (The Pink Pussycat Boutique is a sex shop in the Village. One Atlantic vice president had a house account there, and after sales meetings executives would order sex toys, pornography, and lube, which the boutique delivered.)

By the time I arrived at Atlantic, Ahmet didn't want to be bogged down with the dull details of running the company anymore. He'd been the greatest talent finder in the business, but he had burned out. Now he just wanted to play. He needed an entire entourage to help him function—enablers, drug dealers, hookers, groupies, hangers-on, bodyguards, and yes, his secretary. I became his unofficial cleaner. By the end of the night, his clothes were usually encrusted with cocaine or vomit or both, and he needed a good wiping down. In a way, I'd been training my whole life for the role. It didn't feel that different from taking care of my family, just with more drugs and vomit.

For a normal twenty-five-year-old girl, cleaning puke off an old, drug-addled lecher might have been a deal breaker. I guess I wasn't normal, because I loved it. Ahmet was free. His life was the exact opposite of mine, and I got paid to live some of the wildest parts with him. It knocked me out. How could it not? My mother could barely afford a stuffed animal, and here was a man whose chauffeur drove him in his Mercedes to the company jet. Here was a man who gave Eric Clapton advice and wrote Henry Kissinger letters. He had everything I wanted, but unlike during my childhood, I wasn't on the outside looking in. I was *in*.

Then again, every day gave me compelling reasons to get out. Ahmet ran Atlantic like a dysfunctional family. He created a world of extreme contradiction that could go from fun and exciting one moment to upsetting and abusive the next. When you're new at a job, especially as a woman, you don't know if you can speak up. If you let the first offense go, it becomes much harder to stop the second one from happening. I didn't know where to draw the line, and I didn't even know that a line should or could be drawn. It just seemed normal.

For instance: I'd been on the job a few weeks when I stepped into the elevator with two executives. Somehow, between floors two and one, they pulled my skirt down to the floor. When the elevator doors opened, I faced the crowded lobby in my panties. This was normal.

For instance: every day, senior vice presidents under Doug Morris came into my office and bragged about how big their dicks were, and how great it was going to be for me if I fucked them. They'd brag about each other's dicks too. This was normal.

For instance: many mornings I would open Ahmet's mail to find Polaroid pictures of him naked, performing various sex acts with various women, along with a letter threatening blackmail. This was a rough way to start my day—Ahmet's body looked like a shriveled egg—but for Ahmet, blackmail was as normal as breakfast. It was part of his everyday life. He had protocol for these packages—I'd turn them over to Sheldon, Sheldon would call the girl and get her to sign a nondisclosure agreement, then he'd pay her off from a safe full of cash he kept in his office for just that purpose (this cash, as we'll see, often came from unpaid royalties). This was normal.

I didn't question it. I wasn't even shocked—that's the scary part. Right from the start, I enabled this behavior. The men called me "cunt," "cunty-poo," "blow job." It was against the rules, but again, no one enforced the rules. If you spoke up, you were out. They could replace you in three seconds.

I did take one stand, though. Tunc Erim kept pinching my ass, and I wanted it to stop. Unsure of how Ahmet would take the news, I approached Noreen Woods, Ahmet's retired assistant. Noreen still played a huge role in Ahmet's life. She was like his right hand. She knew every thought he had before he had it. Her entire life was dedicated to him. I hoped, as a woman, she would sympathize with me and fix the situation for me, but she said what I feared she would: "You have to tell Ahmet."

Even though I accompanied Ahmet on his wild nights, he was still an imposing figure. Plus, this guy was sexual harasser number one. What would he say if I told him one of his senior executives touched me in a way I didn't like? I approached him nervously and told him about Tunc.

"Tell him to come in here," Ahmet said.

I buzzed Tunc and said, "Mr. Ertegun wants to see you."

When Tunc entered, Ahmet ripped him a new asshole and made him apologize. Tunc walked out like a dog hit over the head with a newspaper. He never touched my ass again. It was the first time Ahmet stood up for me. I was hooked.

From then on, I'd do anything for Ahmet, even if I knew it was wrong. It started with little lies: "Mrs. Ertegun, Mr. Ertegun won't be home tonight; he's in a closed-door session." Ahmet would pat me on the head and give me a treat—backstage passes to a Genesis concert, where I met Phil Collins.

Then, the lies got bigger:

> "Ahmet would never screw an R&B artist out of royalties."
> "Of course he had lunch five days in a row with Eric Clapton,
> why else would it be on his expenses?"

And bigger:

> "Oh my God, the WEA warehouse was broken into, $1
> million in Atlantic product gone. I wonder who the sus-
> pects are?"
> "We had no knowledge of a merger between our parent
> company, Warner Communications, and Time Inc."

I did more than lie; I also kept Ahmet's secrets. One night, I had to get his signature on some documents, so I ran over to his suite at the Carlyle Hotel. He answered the door wearing a half-open robe and led me into an enormous room complete with a baby grand piano, three scantily clad babes, a table full of cocaine, and several bottles of vodka. Keep in mind, the last time I had to get his signature I found him getting a blow job in a recording studio. This time, I kept my head down as I handed him the papers and a pen. "Look up," he said. "You might see something you like."

The following day, I acted as if nothing had happened, and as my reward, Ahmet invited me to see the Who perform their rock opera *Tommy* for one of his charities. It was a private show, and I got to meet Roger Daltrey and Pete Townshend. Yes, I felt conflicted. I saw many women get used like Kleenex—artists, employees, groupies—and I didn't like it. But that was the price of entry. And let's not pretend it was the hardest price to pay. I was living my dream, answering phone calls all day from the likes of Jimmy Page, Robert Plant, and Mick Jagger, and sometimes partying with them all night. Huge artists were always stopping by the office—one day Melissa Etheridge performed a concert just for us in the conference room. There was no filter between me, as Ahmet's secretary, and the world-famous artists.

In fact, we all had something to gain from helping Ahmet do whatever he wanted, whenever he wanted, at whatever the price. The artists had their careers to think of. I had a career of my own to consider, and after working at Atlantic a few months, I developed a new passion. I wanted to be an A&R executive. That was my price.

A&R stands for "artists and repertoire," and it is one of the most important jobs at a label. A&R executives have a laundry list of duties.

They find and sign talent, and they often help with every phase of making an album, from finding a producer to selecting the songs. If an artist does not write her own songs, the A&R executive works with music publishing companies to find songs for her. The A&R executive is also responsible for managing the recording budget and making sure the studio and musicians get paid. In the boardroom, the A&R executive gets glory for the hits and suffers rejection for the stiffs.

Working in A&R wasn't always my goal, but I could hear their department meetings from my office, and I realized how dumb these guys were and how easily I could do their jobs. Most importantly, I realized that a good A&R executive was almost as important as an artist. Hit records were the lifeblood of any label, and A&R was the pumping heart.

As this goal solidified in my mind, my moral lines became blurred. The voice of Sister Rose Ellen—my conscience, for better or worse— grew fainter. The voice of Ahmet Ertegun—a man with no conscience— replaced it. Some days, when I'd find myself rolling hash joints for Ahmet, or making dominatrix appointments and lying to his wife for him, I'd feel a pang of Catholic guilt. But I quickly learned to rationalize my way around it. After all, didn't Jesus say, "Judge not lest ye be judged"? I had some unusual desires myself, desires that Ahmet encouraged, and I didn't want anyone judging me.

Ahmet made it all seem so natural. He was like the snake in the Garden of Eden charming me with that red, delicious apple. He told me that men couldn't biologically control their sexual urges. He told me that I couldn't expect a man to remain faithful. He told me that my greatest bargaining chip as a woman was my pussy. I believed it because I revered him. I bit the apple.

Meanwhile, my mother was still suffering through radiation treatments. Since we didn't have a car, she had to take the bus to her appointments. My father never went with her. He never asked her how she was doing or tried to support her. In fact, when she got sick, he packed up his things and moved into another bedroom in the house.

I felt helpless and scared for her. The treatment destroyed her stomach, and I spent most of my lunch breaks running to the only supermarket in Midtown, at Fifty-Sixth Street and Sixth Avenue, to buy her food, hoping to find something she could eat. At least I felt I was helping in some way.

Witnessing my mother's sickness made me appreciate the importance of medical benefits. I assumed they came with my job. When my knee started troubling me again, I went to the doctor and learned different. According to Atlantic's Human Resources Department, I was a temp and did not qualify for benefits. I immediately went to Jenny's office. Our friendship had cooled considerably since I had begun working for Ahmet, but she coordinated my benefits, so I had no choice.

"Can I ask you something?" I said.

"What's on your mind?" she asked without looking up.

"Why didn't you tell me that this is a temp position?"

"I wanted to make sure you liked the job before making it permanent," she said.

Total bullshit. Either she arranged the position that way to make the paperwork easier, or she did it to test whether or not Ahmet would like me. I couldn't let the situation stand, but I didn't want to mess with Jenny. As Ahmet's senior assistant, she had more power than I did. Still, I could barely afford to help my mother, let alone pay for the treatment I needed. I decided to go over Jenny's head.

I went into Ahmet's office and said, "I think things have been going well the past few months. Since you haven't said otherwise I assume you're happy with my performance. So I was wondering if you could make my position permanent."

"What are you talking about?" he said.

"I'm a temp."

"You're here every day."

"I know. But I have no health benefits."

"That's ridiculous. Of course your job is permanent."

I left his office happy. This was the second time he stood up for me. Asking Ahmet for help was difficult. I feared him as much as I revered him. He rarely joked or even cracked a smile around me. He let me call him Ahmet in the confines of his office, but in public he was

Mr. Ertegun, and God help me if I forgot it. Even when I'd start to feel rapport building, he'd do something to show how little he trusted me. But after straightening out my health benefits, I felt our relationship beginning to thaw. I had another procedure on my knee, and afterward, I had to walk with a cane for two weeks. Ahmet also walked with a cane, so when he saw me hobble into the office, he said, "Get in here; you're doing it all wrong." He proceeded to give me a physical therapy lesson for half an hour. He held all calls while showing me how to distribute my weight correctly with the cane. He said, "Do it again, do it again," not letting me leave until I had used the cane to his satisfaction.

I decided to return the compassion. He had a water pitcher in his office. It was my job to fill it every day, but I found this demeaning and refused to do it. As a result, a thick layer of dust settled on it. It was a physical manifestation of my resolve. One day, a stifling, ninety-nine-degree day in early July, Ahmet had a tooth pulled. He showed up to work in intense pain. I felt sorry for him, so I washed the pitcher in the kitchen, filled it with ice water, and poured him a glass.

"You drink it first!" he shouted.

I was pissed. *After all the trouble I just went through, this mother-fucker thinks I'm trying to poison him?*

"Forget about me being nice to you ever again!" I yelled.

Ahmet broke into a yellow-toothed grin and laughed. He was busting my balls, a sign of acceptance. I couldn't help but laugh too, but my laughter came from a deeper place than he could know. After a lifetime of feeling rejected, I had finally found a place where I fit, a home, a family. It was a fucked-up family, but at least it was mine.

4

OZ

SUMMER 1987: AHMET CALLED ME into his office.

"Take a letter," he said. "Dear Jew motherfucker . . ."

"That's what you want to say?" I looked at him.

He thought for a moment.

"Okay, delete 'Jew.'"

"Jew motherfucker" was Ahmet's nickname for his archrival, David Geffen. His hatred for Geffen went back many years, and it grew stronger with time, like petrified wood. Geffen was once Ahmet's protégé, but they had a huge falling-out after Ahmet loaned Geffen $10,000 to start his own label. Geffen founded the hugely successful Geffen Records, and he also diversified into film, eventually selling out to MCA Records for triple-digit millions (later, a Japanese conglomerate bought the label and made Geffen a billionaire). Ahmet, on the other hand, had been pressured into selling Atlantic to Warner Bros.-Seven Arts in 1967 for $17.5 million. Even today, the deal is infamous—he practically gave Atlantic away for a song. Ahmet never got over it, and to see Geffen beat him in such spectacular fashion nearly choked him with rage.

During their good years, Ahmet had introduced Geffen to the world of art collecting. Now, as rivals, the two men often battled each other for paintings. On this particular day, Geffen had outbid Ahmet. This was the occasion for the letter. Ahmet continued dictating:

"Go fuck yourself. You fucked with the wrong person. Fuck you. Sincerely, Ahmet M. Ertegun."

He paused.

"Send it."

My relationship with Ahmet grew more fucked up by the day. He was up my ass from nine o'clock in the morning until nine at night, and sometimes later. I got only a half hour for lunch and spent my days chained to a phone in a windowless office. I soon learned never to put Ahmet on hold when he called. Invariably, he'd spend several minutes stuttering and stammering on the phone before he could actually say what he wanted, all while Doug's phone would be ringing off the hook, but I had to stay on the line with Ahmet until he spit it out. He'd give his order and hang up. No "good-bye," no "thank you." I was expected to do his bidding immediately. It was dehumanizing, as if I were his servant.

At the same time, Ahmet became a source of stability. Never mind that the guy could hardly control himself, that he'd fuck in his office or piss in the elevators at Rockefeller Center whenever he got the urge. He became a father figure, giving me the advice and guidance I'd always craved but never got from my own father. I'd come to learn that his advice was, as a rule, terrible, but at least he cared enough to offer it. Ours was a relationship built on extremes.

I realized from the start that Ahmet got what he wanted when he wanted it. I never understood the other executives at Atlantic who didn't seem to comprehend this. For instance, one day Ahmet wanted to buy a refrigerator for his friend Sibel. "Get me that fucking faggot in L.A.," Ahmet ordered. He meant Paul Cooper. Paul was a Doug Morris loyalist and the West Coast general manager. Whatever you needed, he could arrange it. A hooker on the planet Mars at 3:00 AM? Consider it done. Paul Cooper was such an integral part of the company—and so important to Ahmet, Sheldon, and Doug—that when Bette Midler tried to have him fired, they laughed it off.

Sibel lived in L.A., so Ahmet wanted Paul to buy the refrigerator. I called Paul and gave him Ahmet's order.

"What?" Paul said. "We don't do that here."

"OK, Paul. Is that what you want me to tell Ahmet?"

"Yes."

I called Ahmet and said, "Paul Cooper said to tell you that Atlantic Records doesn't purchase refrigerators for your friends."

"Get me that fucking faggot back right now."

I called Paul and connected him to Ahmet. After Ahmet hung up, I buzzed his office and asked him what he had said to Paul.

"I told him to go fuck himself, and he's fired if he doesn't do what I asked."

One refrigerator, coming up.

As I got to know Ahmet better, I became adept at reading his moods. If I saw him getting bored or overwhelmed I'd suggest a trip to the bathroom. That was our code for cocaine. It helped him relax and gave him the energy to function for the long night he was inevitably about to have. Eventually, I felt comfortable enough to put in a few suggestions here and there, and to my surprise, Ahmet occasionally listened to them. Ahmet-fucking-Ertegun, friend of presidents and heads of state, immortal icon in the music business, was listening to *me*. Who could leave a gig like that?

Here it bears repeating that every silver lining at Atlantic came with a massive cloud. My proximity to Ahmet had serious drawbacks. He was an abusive man with a quick fuse. He'd call me stupid when I made a typo, or he'd hurl his favorite insult: peasant. In Ahmet's mind, everyone who worked for him—maybe everyone in the world—was a peasant, except for Doug and Sheldon. Every time he'd berate me, I'd think, *Am I stupid?* That's how he got in your head. Where Doug would charm his way in, Ahmet busted through like a battering ram.

I hated the groupie scene at Atlantic too. The minute one of Ahmet's artists came into town the first order of business was to get them laid. Ahmet would say, "Get the girls," and I'd call through his Rolodex until I found someone ready, willing, and able. These guys would fuck girls young enough to be their daughters without thinking twice. Ahmet took great pride in it, like he was the Turkish sultan offering his concubines.

From the outside, it might be hard to understand why I put up with so much blatant misogyny. I saw no way around it. Even Sylvia Rhone couldn't stop it. Sylvia Rhone was Doug's protégé—an attractive, thin, Wharton School graduate, and one of the first African American women in the business. Soft-spoken and restrained, she rarely revealed her thoughts. In her office she had an anti-apartheid poster of a black man hanging a white man. Needless to say, she scared the men shitless. I didn't envy her. I knew what it meant to work in this business as a woman, but it must have been a special hell to succeed at her level as a woman of color. The business simply had no mold for her.

No one fucked with her, because to fuck with her was to fuck with Doug. She'd pass by my desk every evening at 6:00 PM like clockwork on her way to Doug's office, and they would stay in there long after closing time. Sometimes they would fight just like an old married couple, and they'd get so loud that whoever was left in the office, including Ahmet, would gather outside Doug's door and listen. I don't know what Doug and Sylvia yelled about, but it must have been important. In 1986, Doug promoted her to senior vice president and general manager of the R&B Department, and they have remained close to this day. Sylvia has followed Doug everywhere throughout his career. She now works at Sony with Doug.

But even Sylvia had to put up with the bullshit. For instance, once there was a big meeting with the corporate lawyers. Sheldon, Doug, and Sylvia were there. Other women were present too. Ahmet had just come in for the afternoon—he didn't usually attend meetings, but he saw everyone going into the conference room and followed them—and he started the meeting by saying, "Sheldon, I have to tell you the most remarkable thing." Sheldon, kissing Ahmet's ass as always, said, "Please tell us."

"Last night I went out to a concert," Ahmet said, the whole room hanging on his every word. "Afterward I went backstage with the lead singer and he had five girls lined up naked and we took turns fucking them, one after the other. Pussies are amazing. You're fucking them, and they're a mess, but after we finished, the girls showered and they looked great."

Not one man in the room said a word—they didn't stick up for the women, who shouldn't have had to listen to that story, and the women didn't or couldn't stick up for themselves, including Sylvia.

That was just how the world worked. I once went to a lawyer, who advised me that if I sued for harassment, I'd lose my job. Worse than that, I knew I'd be blackballed from the entire business. Ahmet and his fellow industry heads often disliked or even hated each other, but they'd close ranks to protect their dominion when necessary. I saw male executives get erased that way; who knows what they would have done to a female secretary.

I had no female role models to look to for guidance. No woman had bucked the system and blazed the trail. In all the years I worked there, I saw only one woman stand up for herself. Atlantic distributed Atco Records, and the head of promotion there was cheating with his subordinate. His pregnant wife came to the office with a gun and said, "I'm going to blow your dick off." Talk about blazing a trail. The woman also wrote a letter to corporate, but nothing happened. Her husband and his girlfriend both kept their jobs.

As for me, I needed the job too much to risk it. There's an old joke Woody Allen tells at the end of *Annie Hall*: "This guy goes to a psychiatrist and says, 'Doc, my brother's crazy. He thinks he's a chicken.' And the doctor says, 'Well, why don't you turn him in?' And the guy says, 'I would, but I need the eggs.'"

Why didn't I turn Ahmet in? I needed the eggs.

During those first months on the job, I got a view of Ahmet's family life. Mica came into the office regularly. She'd either meet Sheldon to discuss the Erteguns' finances or she'd run her design business, MAC II. She also stored her jewelry in a vault in the building. Even though she wasn't a great beauty, at least not by the time I met her, she exuded elegance. Everything she wore looked like it cost a million bucks. It probably did—Oscar de la Renta was a close friend.

When Ahmet met Mica in the early 1960s, she was married to a chicken farmer in Canada. Ahmet later said he immediately had to have her, so he broke up her marriage. For decades, they were a formidable couple. They hung out with the Studio 54 crowd in the 1970s—Mick and Bianca Jagger, Halston, Andy Warhol. They attended the same parties as Diana Vreeland and Jackie Onassis. They lived the kind of life I had only read about in *People* magazine. By the time I met them, in the 1980s, Ahmet and Mica had reached a sort of coasting period. They were entering old age—not exactly slowing down, but changing.

Mica had all of Ahmet's aristocratic contempt with none of his warmth. She acted like a real-life Cruella de Vil, more demanding than Ahmet and meaner too. She never smiled, never said hello. We had to call her "Mrs. Ertegun," even to Ahmet. When she'd call, I'd buzz Ahmet and say, "Mrs. Ertegun is on the phone." I once asked Ahmet why he married her, and he said, "She had big tits."

I also met Ahmet's girlfriend, Janice Roeg. Ahmet said that of all the women he dated, Janice was the only one he'd marry. Never mind that he was married to Mica when he said this. It seemed to drive Mica nuts, but in truth, I could see why Ahmet loved Janice. She was tall and had perfect long blonde hair, a pretty face, and a great figure. She was pleasant and nice to everyone she met. Ahmet spoke with Janice on the phone constantly throughout the day, and she picked him up from the office every night. He acted like a kid around her. She could whip him into line with just a few words, and even Mica knew it. Once, when Mica and Ahmet took a vacation in Turkey, he was breaking her balls so bad that Mica called Janice and said, "You have to come to Turkey. I can't handle him." Ahmet even had me sign as a witness on an insurance policy that Janice would receive upon his death—that's how important she was to him.

Many times, I heard Mica complain about Janice at Atlantic events, but she never filed for divorce. She never showed up waving a gun threatening to blow Ahmet's dick off. She stuck around for the enormous wealth and perks that came with being Mrs. Ahmet Ertegun. Like the rest of us, Mica had a price.

Ahmet's older brother Nesuhi also worked at Atlantic as president of WEA International. In many ways, Nesuhi was the exact opposite of Ahmet. He was refined and polite. He had thick hair, wore ascots, and took great pride in his appearance. When he met a woman, he bowed instead of shaking hands. While Nesuhi had taste, Ahmet only had money. For example, Atlantic had an in-house chef who crafted culinary delicacies every day for lunch, but Ahmet would bring in a can of Campbell's tomato soup in a brown bag, plop it on my desk, and tell me to heat it up for him. While Nesuhi dressed impeccably, Ahmet dressed *expensively*. He custom ordered his clothes and bought shoes from John Lobb of London for $2,000 a pair (they even kept a mold of his feet at the store). And yet, he'd walk out of his office with ink all over his shirt. He'd dribble food all over himself while he ate. He wore his pants up to his chest like Kermit the Frog, his fly often unzipped. He was a pig.

Nesuhi's refinement was perhaps the best thing that ever happened to Ahmet. He introduced Ahmet to New Orleans jazz when they were young, and it set the brothers on a musical path for the rest of their lives. Nesuhi's interest never wavered from jazz—he even taught the country's first academic course in jazz at UCLA in the 1950s—but Ahmet ultimately followed the public's tastes. Atlantic followed Ahmet, and the jazz and R&B artists that had built the label receded into the background as rock 'n' roll took over the world. Ben E. King once said, "I think the saddest thing I've ever seen happen is the black music section of Atlantic disappear almost completely. Somewhere along the way, someone stopped paying attention."

That someone was Ahmet.

5

THE CLOWN-FUCKING
AWARDS

IN 1987, AHMET RECEIVED THE Irvin Feld Humanitarian Award from the
National Conference of Christians and Jews. Apparently they didn't know
he was Muslim. I prepared the invitations for the gala dinner, receiving
my first exposure to the rules and regulations of high society. For example,
it seemed strange to address Ahmet's envelope to "Mr. and Mrs. Ahmet
Ertegun," with Mica's name nowhere on the invitation. How could women
gain power, I wondered, if they didn't even get to have names?

The guest list included billionaires like Sid Bass and Edmond Safra
and their wives Anne and Lily, diplomat Francis L. Kellogg and his wife
Mercedes (Sid and Mercedes eventually had an affair, divorced their
spouses, and married each other), Peter Tofu—in short, the whole New
York socialite crowd.

One day, as I worked on the invitations, Kevin Eggers came to visit.
Eggers owned Tomato Records and was one of Ahmet's partners in a
theater investment.

"You look very intent on whatever it is you're doing there," he said.

"Yeah, Ahmet's being honored next month and I'm helping with
the arrangements."

"What's the occasion?"

"The National Conference of Christians and Jews. Ahmet's getting the Irvin Feld Award."

Eggers gave me a strange look. "Irvin Feld started Ringling Bros. and Barnum & Bailey Clown College so he could fuck all the clowns," he said.

"Well, this gig is sounding more prestigious by the minute," I said.

After Eggers left, I went into Ahmet's office and broke the news. "So, I'm getting the clown-fucking award?" Ahmet asked.

"Looks that way."

Ahmet thought for a moment, and a grin spread across his face. It was just his type of award.

I got an invite to the gala—another sign of how close Ahmet and I had become. This was a brave new world for me. My parents had never even taken us to a restaurant, let alone a black-tie gala. I didn't know what to wear, but I knew I didn't have it, so I went shopping. Luckily, I had always loved clothes and I had a good body. I picked out a black dress with a tulle skirt, figuring you can't go wrong with something simple and elegant.

On the night of the gala, I arrived at the Waldorf Astoria on Park Avenue to find the crème de la crème of New York mingling in the ballroom, the men decked out in black ties, the women in gorgeous gowns. Ahmet wore an impeccably tailored tux that probably cost a quarter of my salary. The ballroom buzzed with self-importance. Photographers from every major magazine perched in strategic areas to catch the luminaries unguarded. To accentuate the Irvin Feld theme, the room teemed with clowns, little people, and a contortionist. It made for a bizarre spectacle—the glitterati dressed in formal wear trying to eat dinner while a man stood next to them with his leg bent behind his head.

During the dinner, Ahmet called me to his table. "This is Dorothy, my sec-a-tary," he said. "She told me I'm getting the clown-fucking award." Everyone at the table looked at me like I was an asshole. Mortification burned in my face. *How could Ahmet do that to me?* Mercifully, Henry Kissinger broke the awkward silence by rising to give his speech introducing Ahmet. I couldn't understand a word he said, but I could have kissed him for the distraction. And what a distraction—despite repeated calls from his office warning that under no circumstances would he speak for more than five minutes, the guy wouldn't get off the stage. After twenty minutes of introduction, Ahmet finally got up to accept his award. As he reached the microphone, Kissinger hugged him. Then, dozens of clowns rushed the stage—red noses, face paint, floppy feet, and all. As they surrounded Ahmet and Kissinger, the expression on Ahmet's face was priceless. It almost made up for the way he had embarrassed me.

I should have learned my lesson that night. I had to be careful what I said to Ahmet because he'd invariably repeat it at the most inopportune time. Unfortunately, I made the same blunder when Atlantic general manager Dave Glew left to run Epic Records. Dave wanted to stay at Atlantic, but he wanted a bigger bonus. Ahmet, Doug, and Sheldon each got a $1 million bonus per year, and Dave asked to be cut in. I could hear Ahmet and Sheldon discussing the raise from my office. Ahmet stamped his feet and yelled, "Do you understand, Sheldon, nobody is more important than me? I'm not giving him another cent. Fuck him. Nobody's more important than me." He then called me and said, "Get me what's his name down the hall."

"Which what's his name?" I said.

"You know, the one that wears the suit."

"Mark Schulman? You're going to hire *him*?"

"That's what they're telling me. Just get him."

Mark Schulman was the executive vice president of marketing. When he walked into the office, Ahmet said, "Do you know my secretary doesn't think I should hire you?"

Maybe the clown-fucking award was too good for him.

6

ALL ACCESS

DURING THE SUMMERS, AHMET SPENT seven weeks on vacation in Bodrum, Turkey, leaving me with little to do. Of course, Ahmet's craziness was big enough to reach across the world. Once he asked me to put a case of Clamato juice on the Warner jet and send it to Turkey because they didn't have it there. Another time, when Bob Morgado, president of the Warner Music Group, called to speak with Ahmet, I had to call Turkey and get one of Ahmet's servants to put him on the phone. "Mr. Ertegun, it's Dorothy," I said. Nothing. "It's Dorothy from Atlantic Records." Again, silence. I decided to get more specific: "This is Dorothy from Atlantic Records, the company you founded in 1942." He let out a resounding "*Ohhh.*" It must have been the vodka.

I spent my first summer at Atlantic listening to the A&R meetings going on in Tunc's office across the hall. I considered him my nemesis, but I still wanted to work under him at A&R. Maybe I was crazy. One day, the entire A&R staff had gathered to pick a single for Debbie Gibson's upcoming release. Tunc was screaming at them: "Listen, you motherfuckers, you cocksuckers. Doug wants us to pick this single." After Tunc played the album, the feedback began. As I leaned in to hear the comments, I couldn't believe my ears. I didn't hear a single constructive critique. I knew I could do better than them—hell, at least I couldn't be worse.

After that meeting, an A&R executive named Jason Flom stuck his bushy-haired head into my office and introduced himself. Meeting Jason changed my destiny at Atlantic Records. We became immediate best friends. When I wasn't with Ahmet, I was with him. We never had a sexual relationship, but everyone in the office thought we were dating because we spent so much time together. In reality, we felt like brother and sister.

Jason was a trust-fund baby—the son of Joe Flom, a mergers and acquisitions lawyer at the firm Skadden, Arps, Slate, Meagher & Flom. Joe Flom represented the board of trustees for Warner Communications. Jason, on the other hand, had dropped out of NYU and began working at Atlantic hanging posters. He moved up to an A&R career after signing Twisted Sister. When we met, he was working albums by an artist he had signed named Fiona, as well as a new rock band, White Lion. He had also just returned from a stay at Hazelden, a rehabilitation facility in Minneapolis, making him a triple threat—alcoholic, drug addict, and gambler. I guess I had a type.

In August, I met another man who would change my life and career, when my friend Karen invited me to see Whitesnake with Mötley Crüe at Madison Square Garden. Karen worked for Geffen Records, and she used her expense account to hire a limo to drive us to the show. Inside the limo I met John Kalodner, an A&R executive at Geffen Records. I didn't get to speak much since Karen dominated the conversation, but I was speechless anyway as the limo pulled into the tunnel leading directly underneath the Garden. I'd never even seen a concert at the Garden before, and now I got to ride in like a rock star. *If only the nuns could see me now.*

As we filed backstage, Karen gave me a stick-on pass that read ALL ACCESS. A crowd of people crammed together around a table full of food and drinks waiting for the show to begin. When Mötley Crüe took the stage, I took a spot in the wings and watched the whole show from there. I stood by myself, mesmerized. Most people know what it's like to attend a big rock concert, but few know what it's like to be one of the people onstage facing thousands of screaming fans. That night was particularly exciting because it was the first time Mötley Crüe put drummer Tommy Lee in a rotating cage. I'd never seen such theatrics, and judging by the audience's rabid reaction, I wasn't alone. Mötley Crüe wisely made the rotating cage a regular part of their show.

I got another shock when the show ended. One moment, the building rocked like it was going to explode; the next moment, all eighteen thousand people disappeared. As I stood alone in the deafening silence, John Kalodner caught my eye and walked toward me. He told me he was an A&R man for Geffen Records and had signed Whitesnake. He spoke calmly and slowly with a nasal voice.

"Do you work in the music business?" he asked.

"Yes, at Atlantic Records as Ahmet Ertegun's secretary."

He smiled and said, "I'll be in the building tomorrow. Can I stop by and see you?"

"Sure," I said, "I'll be there glued to my desk all day and probably all night."

Around 2:00 PM the next day, my intercom buzzed. "John Kalodner here to see you," the receptionist said. I told her to send him back and waited in the hall to wave him to my office. We had a short conversation—the phones were ringing off the hook, and Ahmet was about to arrive, so I had to get his mail and messages ready—Kalodner left, and I went back to work thinking nothing of it.

Half an hour later, my intercom buzzed again and I heard that familiar croak ordering me into the office. I found Ahmet sitting at his desk with his hands folded and his glasses resting on top of his head. Before I could ask him what he wanted, he started screaming.

"You had John Kalodner in my office!"

"Yes," I said, wondering how he knew.

"He's an enemy of mine, and an enemy of my company. I should fire you right now."

I was stunned. Ahmet continued yelling: he said Kalodner had worked at Atlantic and took credit for signing acts that Ahmet had signed, like Foreigner and AC/DC. I assured him that Kalodner had not mentioned this.

"Get back to your desk," Ahmet huffed. Then, as I turned to leave, he added a coda to his screaming symphony: "Don't ever see him again."

Like a pissed-off teenager, I planned on doing just the opposite. And I was going to use Ahmet's own words against him. He often told me I had something that all men wanted, and that I could use it as a shortcut to get what I wanted from them. I believed him and figured now was as good a time as any to act on his advice. First, though, I had a score to settle. Back at my desk, I dialed the extension for Geffen Records and asked to speak to John.

"Hello, Bebe," he answered.

I yelled into the phone: "Why didn't you tell me you worked here and that Ahmet hates you? He wants to fire me because you came to my office. You set me up!"

"Can I take you to dinner tonight?" he asked, ignoring my fury.

"Sure," I said, inwardly giddy at disobeying Ahmet. "Let me know where and I'll meet you there. He'll fire me if we're seen together."

I met Kalodner later that evening at the Palm Too restaurant. It was near the UN Plaza Hotel, the only place he stayed on his trips to New York. I still felt upset about what Ahmet had said and kept repeating it like a mantra until Kalodner apologized for the whole incident.

He struck me as abnormal from the start. He had bizarre fixations. Like me, he didn't drink alcohol or do drugs. I asked him what it was like to work A&R for Geffen. He told me about the acts he signed, about working on Aerosmith's comeback album *Permanent Vacation*, and about his huge hits with Whitesnake. He said David Geffen had bought him a Range Rover SUV as a bonus. I couldn't imagine such generosity.

Our first date was fairly standard. We said our goodnights and promised to keep in touch. The next day, he began calling me incessantly to plan our next meeting. Noreen Woods was in that day, and I told her all that had happened. She raised her eyebrows, laughing. She too had been worn out by Ahmet's constant Geffen bashing, and she understood why it felt so good to rebel with Kalodner. She also said she knew a girl who had slept with Kalodner and said he had a big dick.

Hmmmmmmm . . .

7

DOWN UNDER

"Dorothy, it's Chris Murphy calling. How are you, love?"

Chris Murphy managed the band INXS. He was handsome and had perfect manners, along with a pleasing Australian accent. INXS had blown up in Australia, but despite their charismatic and sexy front man, Michael Hutchence, and several radio-ready rock songs with solid hooks from their previous albums, they had yet to break in America. They'd just recorded a new album, *Kick*, and Atlantic didn't want to release it. According to *Rolling Stone*, after listening to it for the first time, Doug offered the band $1 million to record another album, saying, "This is shit." The band believed in it, and Chris Murphy set up a secret meeting with Andrea Ganis, the VP of Top 40 promotion, to get the singles on the radio. Meanwhile, he booked a college tour on the band's dime. The album started to take off, and Atlantic relented, inviting the band to America for a huge release party.

We also had a new tool to break INXS, one that had not been available in the past: MTV. MTV was only a few years old, but music videos were already competing with radio play for the ultimate power to break a band. MTV had several advantages. If a radio station played a song, say, in New York, it only reached one market. If a video played on MTV, it reached the entire country. Also, MTV played the videos on a loop all day. In short, it was a marketer's dream.

Because INXS was such a visual band, MTV was the perfect medium for them. The band had made a deal with Joel Schumacher, director of *St. Elmo's Fire* and *The Lost Boys.* In return for appearing on the *Lost Boys* soundtrack, Schumacher would direct the video for the new INXS single, "Devil Inside." (The video was nominated for Best Editing at the 1988 MTV Video Music Awards, losing to another INXS single, "Need You Tonight"/"Mediate.")

"Any updates from Joel?" Chris asked.

"No, I haven't heard from him," I said. "As soon as I get the schedule for the shoot, I'll fax it over."

"Thanks, love."

A few days later, Atlantic began gearing up for the *Kick* release. The office hummed with energy. Pins, T-shirts, photos, and jackets, all with the *Kick*/INXS logo on them, lay strewn about. Atlantic had booked Rockefeller Center for the release party, complete with a performance by INXS in the courtyard where they set up the ice skating rink at Christmas.

I should have felt excited, but I was dizzy from the constant clanging of the phone. It rang again, and I answered. As I said my normal "Ahmet Ertegun's office," I felt a presence standing in my doorway. I looked up and saw Michael Hutchence in all his glory. He motioned to me that he wanted to smoke, and I waved him in, pointing to my chair. He closed my door behind him and sat down. I hung up the phone, my heart pounding.

"I'm Dorothy, Mr. Ertegun's secretary."

"I'm—" he started, but I cut him off.

"I know who you are!"

Michael had grown his hair long, a change from his look in the video for the band's previous single, "What You Need." He had large brown eyes, just like me. He had high cheekbones, just like me. His body was thin like mine. His lips were impossibly full. He wore jeans and a black T-shirt and spoke with a bewitching accent. I had never seen a man so beautiful.

Michael took out a cigarette, and I lit it for him. I told him I loved the videos for "Need You Tonight" and "Mediate." I even began to sing:

"Mediate, hallucinate, love your mate." He laughed and smiled at me. Clearly, I couldn't hold a note.

Michael sat quietly smoking, but I had work to do. Ahmet had requested that I mail some promotional CDs, so I went to the cabinet to get them. As I struggled on my tippy-toes to get the CDs from the top shelf, I felt Michael on my back leaning with his arm on me to reach them for me. I slowly turned around and our eyes met. Both of us were grinning and breathing hard.

We separated, and he said he had to be getting back or they would all come looking for him. I could barely speak so I just smiled and waved. He opened the door, and just like that, he was gone. I fixed my skirt and thought, *Holy shit, this is the greatest job ever.*

Then, as if to ruin the mood, Tunc walked in.

"You were blowing Michael Hutchence in here?" he said.

"I was not," I said. "Why don't you blow him?"

"Maybe I will. He's so pretty."

"Don't you have any work to do?" I said. "Doesn't Phil Collins need a manicure? Doesn't Julian Lennon need some coke?"

"Why are you so nasty?" he asked.

"Why are you a degenerate?" I shot back.

Tunc turned white. I didn't understand it. He couldn't possibly care what I said about him. Then I saw Michael standing in the hallway. He'd heard everything we said. He walked back toward us and spoke to Tunc in an authoritative tone.

"Say you're sorry to her right now, or I will make you say it," Michael said. "She's a lady; don't talk to her that way."

What? I was a lady? I had never heard anyone in the music business call me that before. *My hero!* The feeling of a man sticking up for me was new and exciting. It made me feel important. It also turned me on.

"I'm sorry," Tunc said, sheepishly.

I stuck my tongue out at him. Ahmet came whipping around the corner and stopped to greet Michael. He never stopped to talk to an employee—that is, a peasant—but he always lit up when he saw one of his artists. He shook Michael's hand and whispered, "Come by my office after you're done. I got hash."

Ahmet went into his office, and the dreaded intercom on my desk buzzed.

"Come in here," he said.

I picked up the mail folders, my steno pad, and his pile of messages, and went in. Ahmet was sitting back in his chair with his glasses on his head.

"You were talking to Michael?"

"Yes."

"About what?"

I told Ahmet that he came into my office for a cigarette and that was it, but I was talking fast, almost out of breath. Ahmet sensed my excitement. He leaned back even more in his chair, clasped his hands, and had me light a cigarette for him. He sat for a moment deep in thought, a signal that he was about to have another of his brilliant ideas. Ahmet gave bad advice, yes, but his ideas were the stuff legends are made of. His latest brilliant idea was to start the Rock & Roll Hall of Fame. He was in talks with famed architect I. M. Pei to build it in Cleveland. I couldn't wait to hear what he was cooking up for me.

He repeated the information I had given him, building his case like a prosecutor: "Michael came into your office to smoke a cigarette. You talked to each other for a while. You clearly liked it." It was dangerous to show emotion in front of Ahmet—any sign of weakness let him know how he could fuck with you. Try as I might, though, I couldn't hide my delight. I nodded at everything he said. Ahmet thought a moment longer and gave his verdict: "You should go out with him."

No shit, Ahmet. He's a hot, rich singer. I'd like to marry him! Of course, I didn't say that. Instead, giggling, I said, "I don't think I'm pretty enough for him. He's beautiful." I always felt extremely insecure about my looks, especially around a good-looking man.

Ahmet replied, "You'll do. Besides, why did God give you a pussy if you're not going to use it?" Disregarding the crudity, I thought it was one of his better ideas. As soon as I got back to my desk, Ahmet's line lit up.

"Ahmet Ertegun's office," I said.

"Is this Dorothy?" the voice said.

"Speaking," I said, smiling at the Australian accent.

"This is Michael Hutchence."

"Oh, hi, Michael. I'll get Ahmet."

"Actually, I called for you. Care to meet me for a drink after you get finished with work?"

"Oh . . . sure," I said casually, as if I had rock stars calling every day with similar offers. "Meet me on the Fifty-First Street side of the building at nine o'clock. And by the way . . . call me Bebe."

8

LUCKY SPERM

EVEN THOUGH I WAS MEETING exciting men, I felt unfulfilled answering Ahmet's phones. I knew I'd never earn anyone's respect that way, not even Ahmet's. That Christmas, I received a bonus of twenty-five dollars (Geffen gave Kalodner a new car just for signing one band). I also got a pair of earrings from Ahmet and a pair of earrings from Doug. The earrings came from a woman named Jacqueline, who spent hours in Doug's office. I don't know what they did in there, but I don't think Doug was that interested in women's jewelry.

The earrings would have been a nice gesture, but they were bought with company money. Also, I didn't have pierced ears. Despite spending all day with me for months, neither Ahmet nor Doug noticed, and most likely, neither one cared.

I wanted to be where the action was. Maybe that's why I liked John Kalodner. He had my dream job, signing big bands and hobnobbing with industry elites, and he didn't seem to discount me just because I was a secretary. I headed west to spend New Year's Eve 1987 with him.

As a young woman, I was ready to go sexually. I didn't need foreplay. I learned quickly, though, that men in the music business didn't have normal sex—they had to have drugs, toys, pornography, and multiple people involved. All they talked about was what they were doing next, what acts, what groups, what positions.

Kalodner was extremely rigid and compulsive. Everything revolved around him and what he liked. We cared about each other, but on a superficial level, with a hypocritical display of pretend devotion. I knew he could help my career, and the myth about his prowess was true. He was good in bed. Narcissists usually are.

I liked quirky people, and Kalodner was about as quirky as you could get without needing medication. He wore a white suit every day, with round glasses and shoulder-length hair, modeling his appearance after John Lennon's *Let It Be* period. At restaurants, he ordered only chicken and Coke, which had to come in a bottle. If they only had Coke in cans, he made a huge fuss until someone from the restaurant went out and found a Coke in a bottle. This made me uncomfortable at first, because I hate when people are obnoxious to waiters, but I realized he wasn't trying to be a jerk. He was just a prima donna, worse than Ahmet or any artist I ever knew.

He complained about everything. He complained he didn't make enough money. He complained about the other A&R guys at Geffen. He complained his ass didn't get kissed enough. He had two assistants who ran his entire professional and personal life. They did his banking, washed his cars, and took care of his dry cleaning. He was a real hotshot at Geffen, and he knew it. As a perk of his indispensability, Geffen let him expense everything: meals, gifts, you name it.

In his defense, Kalodner worked hard. He had no formal musical training and no college degree, but he could determine from demos which songs were hits, envision the arrangements, and help the band nail the tracks in the studio. He was an artistic force. Still, being with him was like dating the Queen of England. I had grown up believing the world owed me nothing. Kalodner, like Ahmet, seemed to think the world owed him more than everything. Where Ahmet called people peasants, Kalodner called people cretins.

He appreciated that I paid for my own modest lifestyle—although he had enough money to last a few lifetimes, and I made $23,500 a year, I never asked for financial help. Even as a child, I hated the feeling of anyone having power over me. As an adult, I felt hell-bent on making sure I didn't owe any man anything. Kalodner liked to show off his wealth, though, and he spared no expense trying to impress me—fine dining, Cartier jewelry, Four Seasons hotels. I have to admit it worked.

He hated New York, so if I wanted to see him, it meant fantasy trips to Los Angeles or parts unknown, which I happily took. On these trips I met and mingled with the biggest names in the business. Kalodner was at the height of his career at Geffen—he'd signed Whitesnake, Aerosmith, Wang Chung, Cher, and the Christian artist Michael W. Smith, and had huge success with each. Every songwriter, producer, manager, and artist wanted to hang with him. I guess I wasn't so different from those hangers-on. I knew he could help my career, just like they did. But I also contributed. I introduced Kalodner to Diane Warren, an up-and-coming songwriter who went on to win a Grammy, an Emmy, and a Golden Globe, and earn eight Academy Award nominations. He recognized her talent, and I felt justified—I had a good ear.

We had an open relationship; he just forgot to tell me. A few weeks after we started dating, he announced his need for complete honesty, and after that, every time he fucked a girl, he phoned to tell me. After receiving a few dozen phone calls full of "complete honesty," I told Kalodner to go fuck himself. I said, "I'm calling you the next time I go fuck someone, and I'll make sure it's someone big." He threw a tantrum and told me I wasn't allowed to fuck anyone else. He expected me to put up with his bullshit and love it.

Despite my hard-ass act with Kalodner, he had hurt me. I sought advice from Larry Yasgar, the VP of dance music and single sales at Atlantic. Normally, I would have gone to Ahmet, but he had forbidden me from even speaking to Kalodner. So I explained the situation to Larry—how Kalodner fucked around and called me after each girl, how he expected me to remain faithful regardless, even how he nagged me for a threesome with one of Jason's artists on Atlantic, Fiona Flanagan. He sent me a photo of a new 1988 Jaguar with a note attached that said, "This could be yours if you eat pussy—JDK."

Larry read the note and said, "He's a real beauty. They don't make 'em like this anymore." He then pointed between my legs and said, "Kid, that thing can't talk. Men have no idea how many other men you fuck. Please tell this sick fuck to go fuck himself."

I didn't tell Kalodner to fuck off; instead, I helped him realize his sexual fantasies—without me. Jason had a heavy metal act called Manowar, fronted by a nice Italian guy named Joey DeMaio. DeMaio was a true gentleman, and he treated me like his kid sister. If not for the wild mane of hair cascading down his back, you'd think he swept floors at a grocery store. In terms of pussy, though, DeMaio was on the Gene Simmons level. A threesome for him was just a party that hadn't started yet. He liked fivesomes, sixsomes, or more—we're talking full-on orgies. From what I heard, at these orgies he played the role of director, telling the girls what to do, where to do it, and in what combinations. Kalodner was in awe of him.

I told Joey DeMaio about my problems with Kalodner—that he wanted me to have a threesome, but I wasn't interested—and DeMaio said, "You should introduce him to me. If you don't want to do it, why deprive him of fulfilling his sexual needs?" The way he explained it made so much sense. I introduced them with a simple message: "You two fucking belong together."

At the time, Manowar was huge in Europe but couldn't find an American audience. DeMaio wanted his next album to put the group over in America, and he wanted out of his contract at Atlantic. Maybe it had something to do with the time Doug told him, "I was a songwriter. I know what it's like to eat hot dogs. Why can't you guys write a song about sex? Do you know anything about it?" Jason didn't want to let the band go, though. Manowar was one of his most important groups, precisely because of their European success. He and Joey used to argue about it, until one day, Joey came into Jason's office and showed him a photo of himself jumping out a plane. He said, "If I'm crazy enough to do that, I'm crazy enough to jump out this window—but I'm not going alone." Jason went downstairs and talked to Doug. He came back a while later and released Manowar.

Kalodner swooped in for the kill. He gave DeMaio a million-dollar contract with Geffen—this was back when a million dollars was still a million dollars—and the two libertines fucked their way around the world. They went everywhere, from SeaWorld to Communist Russia, fucking housewives who were bored with their lives. They'd take these women for manicures, buy them nice dinners, and give them a glimpse of life through the rock 'n' roll looking glass. If these guys had to choose between sex and food, they'd starve. And if a woman got in trouble, no mountain was too high and no valley too deep to stop them from rushing to her rescue. Take for example the story of a groupie attached to Slash, the guitarist in Guns N' Roses. DeMaio banged her, and then Kalodner invited her to L.A. to bang her. She was eventually arrested on a drug charge and thrown in an Arizona jail. Kalodner regularly visited her. Some of the A&R guys wrote her letters, and they may have visited her too. They all wrote letters to the judge on her case asking for leniency.

Meanwhile, for orchestrating DeMaio and Kalodner's debauchery—which, by the way, made DeMaio a millionaire—I didn't even get a bouquet of flowers. In fact, I got dumped. I visited Kalodner in L.A. on Columbus Day weekend, and when I got home I called to check in, but he never returned the call. A few days later, he sent a box of my personal effects. He refused any closure or even an explanation. He just cut me off. It hurt. Despite the fucked-up things that had happened between us, I cared about him.

My relationship with Jason Flom ran much more smoothly, maybe because there was no sex involved. Also, his stay in rehab made him docile. One of the first things they make addicts do in rehab is clean the toilets. It humbles you. Of course, humility has its limits. Like Ahmet and Kalodner, Jason was a lucky sperm, blessed by an accident of birth, and like them, he gave me another lesson on what life was like when you had money. Not long after I met Jason, the bank took his credit cards away. This posed a problem—when employees traveled, we had to charge expenses on our own cards and then the company would reimburse us later. Jason called his dad, and his dad called Jim Robinson, then CEO of American Express, who also happened to be a client of Skadden, Arps, Slate, Meagher & Flom. Within hours, Jason received a new American Express card, hand delivered by a messenger.

Jason was different from the other rich pricks in important ways, though. He didn't yet know his power. He was awkward with girls and had a quick sense of humor to deflect uncomfortable situations. I felt like he was my little brother and made it my mission to protect him. We could spend all day together and never tire of each other. He called me "Little Honey," and I called him "Big Honey." He took me to all the best restaurants near our office in Rockefeller Center and expensed them all. That impressed me. Apparently, on Jason's level, there was such a thing as a free lunch.

Jason was one of Doug's projects. Doug liked to hire the relatives of wealthy, influential people, turn them into his protégés, and use their family connections to help his career. Doug also loved people who shared his Ivy League education (Doug went to Columbia). He sent Jason to rehab, curing his alcohol, drug, and gambling addictions. After that, whenever Doug needed help with his contract or the powers at corporate, Joe Flom stepped up.

To show just how far these relationships went, in 1989 Warner merged with Time Inc. to create Time Warner, the world's largest media conglomerate. Joe Flom acted as one of the attorneys for the merger. Before the merger was announced in the press, I noticed that several high-level executives at Atlantic were buying new luxury cars, including a Bentley and a BMW.

I cringed at the blatant dishonesty and immorality of the ways these men scratched each other's backs. To me, it was another example of how the rich protected each other and helped each other grow and maintain wealth, breaking the law with near impunity, while the rest of us stayed down in the trenches.

9

LUCKY CRIMINALS

EVERY MAJOR LABEL BROKE THE law in some way; Atlantic was just better at it than most. As one top Atlantic executive admitted, "All we did was fuck and steal." The level of greed and disrespect—for the law and the artists—was jaw dropping. These men were multimillionaires, and yet they still lusted for more and would do anything to get it. Of course, when someone else needed something, they turned into misers. One day, my pen ran out of ink and I went to Sheldon's office to ask for some new office supplies. He said, "We don't have money for pens; use a pencil." He wasn't kidding.

After working at Atlantic for a few months, I gave these men a nickname: lucky criminals. Here's how they did it: Perhaps the most common crime was "payola," the practice of paying for radio play. After the infamous payola scandal of the early 1960s, which ruined Alan Freed's career (and almost ruined Dick Clark), the practice slowed, but it never stopped. By the 1980s, it had morphed into a new business model, the "independent promoter." This promoter was essentially a payola middleman. Instead of giving money straight to a DJ, a record label would give it to the promoter, who would approach the DJ and get the song played. Some of these promoters would kick back cash to the department heads, enabling them to take vacations over the Christmas holidays to Hawaii and Aspen. Some got Gucci loafers or cash to fund second homes. The list goes on.

The best of these promoters soon formed a loose alliance called the Network. It was estimated that major labels shelled out $40 million a year to the Network and other independent promoters in the early 1980s. They had no choice. In 1979, CBS's Columbia Records tried and failed to get radio play without the Network (CBS alone paid nearly $10 million a year for promotion). Pink Floyd had just released "Another Brick in the Wall," their first single in years. They had scheduled a huge concert in California to open their world tour. Banking on the power of Pink Floyd's name and the upcoming concert, Columbia directly approached a few California radio stations. Not a single station played the song. As the day of Pink Floyd's concert neared and the record still hadn't received airplay, someone at Columbia wised up and paid an independent promoter. Within weeks, the single hit number two on the *Billboard* Hot 100 chart.

Another way Atlantic manipulated sales was to create a gold record by sleight of hand, or more accurately, sleight of paperwork. If a record wasn't performing, Atlantic would wait until the end of the month, when we reported sales to the RIAA, and convince the big retailers to order enough copies for the record to go gold. Once these orders came in, Atlantic would report the numbers, and the RIAA would certify the record gold. The next day, the retailers would send in their returns and get a refund. The product never even left the warehouse. Had the RIAA looked over Atlantic's books, they might have come up with a new certification for these albums—fool's gold.

The most common practice, however, and the most serious one, was not paying royalties to artists. Atlantic did this in various ways under the free-goods clause. Every record contract had a free-goods clause, and it was nonnegotiable. Only Led Zeppelin and the Rolling Stones, as far as I know, were powerful enough to avoid it. In theory, free goods were supposed to be promotional materials the label gave away to radio DJs and other tastemakers to support a project—they weren't for sale and thus weren't reported for royalties or taxes. In practice, however, free goods were used as a shelter for several different forms of royalty theft.

One method of royalty theft was selling "cut-outs." A cut-out is an album that has gone out of print, usually because it didn't sell out its run. Atlantic would take the remaining physical copies and mark them (on LPs, they'd literally cut out a notch on the jacket, hence the name), then sell these cut-outs to a middleman for pennies on the dollar. It might not seem like much, but those pennies added up, and there was money yet to be made. The middleman would sell the cut-outs to retail stores, where the records ended up in bargain bins. Atlantic took a percentage of the bargain-bin sales, and because they called these records free goods, they paid no royalties or taxes on the income.

Another method of royalty theft was "overruns." When the pressing plant printed more LP jackets than records, Atlantic would order extra vinyl to fill the empty jackets. Atlantic would give these overruns to retailers, who, again, sold them in bargain bins. Just like with cut-outs, Atlantic made money from these sales without paying royalties or taxes. Unlike with cut-outs, overruns often came from popular albums, making them much more lucrative for the label. For instance, if the plant printed too many sleeves for Genesis's *Invisible Touch*—an album that went six times platinum (a platinum album is awarded for one million sales) in America and four times platinum in the United Kingdom— Atlantic could make millions of dollars in pure profit from overruns. If you walked into the record store in 1986, you'd see *Invisible Touch* on the shelf for $12.99, and you'd find the same album in the "G" section of the bargain bin for $5. If you bought the bargain-bin record, Genesis got screwed.

The worst offense, and, according to the *L.A. Times*, the one that would eventually bring down Doug Morris, was selling what we called "cleans." Unlike cut-outs, which had once been regular retail items, and unlike overruns, which were by-products of a commercial record, cleans were meant strictly for promotion. This was the true purpose of the free-goods clause. They were supposed to be capped at a certain number, per the record contract. Naturally, Atlantic abused this system. They'd funnel cleans to retailers, who sold them at full price, and by now, you can probably guess the rest of the story. Atlantic made millions, paid no taxes, and shafted the artist.

By selling cut-outs and cleans with no intent to pay the artist, Atlantic was in breach of its own contracts, and the label committed fraud, a criminal act. The stakes for being caught were high. Throughout the mid-1980s, MCA Records was caught up in a public FBI investigation for the same shady business practices used at Atlantic. Ultimately, Irving Azoff's name was dragged through the mud as he and MCA were connected to several powerful mobsters, including Sal Pisello, who sold MCA's cut-outs. Pisello was sentenced to four years in prison and a $250,000 fine.

For an artist or a manager, the only defense was to audit the company on your own dime. Good managers, like Led Zeppelin's Peter Grant, did just that, constantly auditing Atlantic and often turning up small fortunes in back royalties. But most managers stopped paying attention immediately after signing the contract, and the powers at Atlantic knew this. They'd soothe these managers into a false sense of security. "Forget the free-goods clause," they'd say. "Look at the final number you're putting in your pocket after the record sales, the tour, the merchandising. If you're not happy with that number, we'll make it up to you." CDs were so profitable, the bands and their managers made millions of dollars, never suspecting that millions more were being skimmed off the top. With all the sex, drugs, and cash, who had time for an audit?

That's not all. Atlantic also used cleans from successful artists to boost underperforming acts. Here's how it worked (this is a fictional example, but it gives the basic setup of the crime): Say we had two albums out at the same time—one from Laura Branigan and one from INXS. We knew Branigan wouldn't sell much and that INXS would sell in the millions. To help Branigan's record, Atlantic would direct the sales staff to offer INXS cleans to big retailers such as Sam Goody and Tower Records, as well as the smaller stores we called "mom and pops." There was one catch: to get the cleans, they had to buy Branigan's album. This was a good deal for the stores—they got free high-selling merchandise, and all they had to do in return was stock an album that probably wouldn't sell too well (if necessary they could return unsold copies at the end of the month). It was a good deal for Branigan—her album would succeed on the INXS bump. It was a raw deal for INXS, but unless their manager audited the company, they'd never know they'd been exploited and not paid royalties.

With so much money being made off the books, Atlantic was awash in illegal cash. This cash was often used to fund more questionable activities—payola, drugs, gambling. Once some high-level executives reportedly dropped $29,000 on hookers at a WEA convention. That money came from unpaid royalties. Ahmet also used cash from cleans to pay off women who tried to blackmail him. Time Warner looked the other way as they reaped huge profits and the executives collected large bonus packages and lucrative contract renewals.

Even the legal shit we did was messed up. Every time we did anything for an artist—whether it was booking studio time or spending money on promotion—we submitted a "charge-back," which would be taken from the artist's royalties. Promotion people would travel around the country to push a song, wining and dining radio DJs, spending the artist's money lavishly. Then there was video promotion, manufacturing, production, and studio time. The artist paid for all of this. Sometimes they even paid for their own gifts—Doug once bought Debbie Gibson a baby grand piano and charged it back to her. Again, unless artists audited the company, they had no idea how their money was actually being spent.

Eventually the hammer would fall, but as often happens in corporate America, the punishment was nominal—a few figureheads rolled while the underlying corruption went untouched. We'll get to that. For now, consider this: if the top brass at Atlantic didn't care about screwing the very people who made them rich, what chance did I have?

10

FOLLOW THE YELLOW
BRICK ROW

I STILL WANTED TO WORK in A&R, but I knew I'd never make it unless I forced the issue. During one of my lunches with Jason, I concocted a plan. Jason had gained some momentum with White Lion—MTV was playing the video to their single "Wait"—but he couldn't get the band on tour with a big act. At the same time, Aerosmith released *Permanent Vacation* on Geffen Records, and it caught fire, eventually going five times platinum. I knew that Aerosmith had a world tour planned to support the album. It didn't take a genius to know which strings to pull.

Kalodner was good friends with Aerosmith's manager, Tim Collins. He'd even introduced me to Tim. So one night I invited both Jason and Kalodner to dinner. As the two men circled each other, I flat out asked Kalodner if he could talk Tim into putting White Lion on the *Permanent Vacation* tour. Kalodner agreed. I was stunned—another rich older guy was listening to me. Maybe Ahmet was right about the power of pussy.

Part of White Lion's promotional campaign involved sending giant stuffed lions to radio DJs and asking them to add "Wait" to their play-lists. We sent one of the lions and a tape to Tim, and he offered White Lion a slot opening for Aerosmith, easy as that. Within a few months, White Lion's album went double platinum.

Ahmet celebrated the success as much as I did. He hated Kalodner and Geffen, but he loved money more. And he needed a hit. In recent years Atlantic had taken a nosedive and struggled to stay afloat, surviving on the strength of its back catalog and Larry's Dance Department, with hit acts like Nu Shooz, Stacey Q, and Debbie Gibson. Atlantic also distributed Island Records and Virgin Records, giving Ahmet access to groups like U2 and Melissa Etheridge, and all the money they brought in. But as far as rock 'n' roll went, Geffen reigned supreme with Guns N' Roses, Whitesnake, and Sonic Youth along with a who's who of established stars like Elton John, Joni Mitchell, and Peter Gabriel. Geffen continued to beat Atlantic into the 1990s, signing Nirvana, Weezer, and Beck, among others. Ahmet couldn't compete with Geffen, but with White Lion, he could at least keep his nemesis in sight.

To celebrate White Lion's success, we had a party after the band's show at Madison Square Garden. The whole company was there. Ahmet and Jason presented the band with a platinum album, and then they surprised me with a platinum album of my own. Ahmet even made a speech about me. For those who could read between the lines, Ahmet was praising me for fucking Kalodner and getting the Aerosmith tour out of it—he said things like, "This is a girl who goes above and beyond." I proved I could play the game by his rules and at a high level, and it changed the way he saw me.

Jason shared Ahmet's excitement, and as my best friend, he shared the credit, telling Doug what I had done. A few days later, Doug came in to get his messages and told me how highly Jason spoke of me. He said he'd keep an eye on me, and that I might be the first to go from a secretarial desk to the A&R Department.

I felt like I had been given the key to a secret club.

With Doug now in my corner, along with Jason and Kalodner, I felt closer than ever to A&R. I just needed a break, and it wasn't long in coming. A few days after the party for White Lion, Jason dashed into my office. He had just come from an AA meeting with Steve Pritchett, a manager in Doc McGhee's New York office. Doc managed Mötley Crüe and Bon

Jovi, among others, and according to Pritchett, he had just signed a new band called Skid Row. Skid Row had an upcoming show at Birch Hill, a club in Sayreville, New Jersey. "You're going with me," Jason insisted. "It will be worth it."

During the ride to Jersey, Jason filled me in on the details—the band was a side project of Jon Bon Jovi. What he said next nearly knocked me out: Bon Jovi was taking Skid Row on tour as their opening act.

This was huge. Bon Jovi's third album, *Slippery When Wet*, had just come out, and on the back of such mammoth singles as "Wanted Dead or Alive," "Livin' on a Prayer," and "You Give Love a Bad Name," the album went twelve times platinum. Skid Row now had my full attention.

I got even more excited when we arrived at the club. Jason and I squeezed into the packed crowd and stood surrounded by hundreds of Jersey girls (and guys, for that matter) who were ravenously awaiting showtime. As soon as the lead singer took the stage, I knew why. Skid Row's front man, Sebastian Bach, was one of the most beautiful men I'd ever seen. He wasn't my type—way too pretty—but I could see he was absolutely breathtaking, nonetheless. He stood a lean six foot three, with a mane of blond hair, high cheekbones, and lips so pouty and full they belonged on a Victoria's Secret model. Bottom line: he was a star.

"Are you going to try and sign them?" I asked Jason on the way back to the city.

"It won't happen," he said. "They're already in talks with Geffen."

He didn't need to say more. Atlantic couldn't—or wouldn't—compete with Geffen financially. Ahmet acted like every band he signed was taking his personal money. David Geffen, on the other hand, never hesitated to throw money at a band. He'd spend twice what Ahmet would.

The next day I called Kalodner to tell him about the Skid Row show. He knew about them, and he told me Doc was in talks with Tom Zutaut, the A&R executive at Geffen responsible for signing Tesla and Guns N' Roses. The paperwork was all but drawn up. So now I knew the situation. If I wanted to reach A&R status, I had to do the impossible: get Ahmet to spend money, and fast.

Kalodner said he had been invited to dinner at Bon Jovi's house in New Jersey, and he asked me to join him. Maybe he wanted to help my career, or maybe he just didn't see me as a threat. I played it cool.

Dinner with Jon Bon Jovi and a chance to find out more about Skid Row? No big deal.

Bon Jovi lived in Rumson, a wealthy New Jersey suburb, in a modest but nice house (smaller than the French château–style mansion he has now). He was handsome and friendly as he greeted us at the door and introduced us to his girlfriend (and future wife), Dorothea Hurley. Kalodner split off with Jon to talk about Skid Row while I got to know Dorothea. She seemed warm and down to earth, with a natural beauty that was simple without being plain. She and Jon were high school sweethearts and, as I learned during our conversation, she was a martial arts champion. Any other night, I would have loved to learn more about her, but on this night, I couldn't help but give half my attention to Kalodner's discussion with Jon.

The doorbell sounded and Richie Sambora entered with *Playboy* model Ashley Lahua. After a few more cocktails, we moved into the dining room, where Dorothea served a delicious, home-cooked macaroni dinner.

"So what's it like working for Ahmet?" Jon asked. Even he wasn't immune to the Ahmet Ertegun mystique.

"Let's just say, everything you've heard is true," I said.

That got some laughs, but I wasn't joking. As dinner progressed, the guys at the table seemed more interested in talking about my job answering Ahmet's phone than their careers as rich and famous rock stars.

"I heard Ahmet can out-party Zeppelin," Jon said.

"That's how he signed the Stones," someone added.

This was true—Ahmet had signed the Rolling Stones to Atlantic in 1971. At the time, every label wanted the band, but Ahmet wanted them more: he was enamored with Mick Jagger; he wanted to be Mick Jagger; I think he even wanted to fuck Mick Jagger. Mick seemed to take priority over everyone in Ahmet's life, even Mica. Ahmet would carry on about Mick to the point where I thought he was in love with him. Ahmet was also an alcoholic, a drug abuser, and a sexual maniac. As it turned out, this worked in his favor with the Stones. After a night of hard partying, Mick finally told Ahmet that the Stones wanted to sign with Atlantic. Ahmet fell asleep while he was talking. Later, Ahmet said of the incident, "I think the fact that I fell asleep while he was telling me they wanted to go on Atlantic absolutely solidified the deal because in his mind he thought, *This is a guy who doesn't give a shit.*" When it came time to sign the contract, legend has it that Ahmet was so trashed on bourbon he fell out of his chair.

While everyone marveled at Ahmet's drunken coup with the Stones, I kept a close eye on Jon's reaction. He was so fascinated by Ahmet that I realized I might be able to use him to help steer Skid Row to Atlantic. Yes, money was a major roadblock, but the buzz about Skid Row was so strong I knew I had to try to make something happen. I believed in the band, but more importantly, I believed in myself. The time had come to leave my secretarial desk behind.

After dinner, we sat around playing cards. I waited until Kalodner was busy talking to Richie Sambora, then I approached Jon.

"You know, Ahmet would love to meet you," I said.

"Man, that guy's a legend," Jon said dreamily.

Yes, Ahmet sure was a legend. And I'd just thrown down the only card I had to play.

"You should talk to him about Skid Row," I said. "I've seen him break a band. When he believes in a project, there's no greater force in the business."

As Jon and I talked, Kalodner caught my eye. He smiled imperceptibly, so no one else in the room would notice. He knew I was trying to edge him out of the deal but his ego was too big to worry about it. Besides, he had so many notches on his A&R belt that Skid Row hardly mattered to him.

At work the following Monday, I buzzed Jason's office. "Can you stop by my desk?"

"I have a ten o'clock with Doug. Can it wait until lunch?"

"No. Hurry up."

Doug's line rang. "Doug Morris's office," I said.

"Hey, Dorothy, it's Toby. Is Doug around?"

"No." I hung up. That annoying fuck was the last thing I needed.

Toby Emmerich was a rich kid who started at Atlantic shortly after I did. Despite Ahmet's fervent "You must start at the bottom" speech at my job interview, I watched him hire Toby right into A&R off the street with no experience. Ahmet wanted a painting from the André

Emmerich Gallery on Fifty-Seventh Street, and André Emmerich was Toby's father. On Toby's first day, he was fast-tracked straight to Tunc's office for A&R prep: "Listen, you motherfucker, you'll get a credit card and an expense account, and Doug will approve your travel." It pays to have a rich father.

Toby nauseated me. I guess it wasn't his fault, but he was a daily reminder that only women (and I guess men without connections) had to start at the bottom. It didn't help that Toby was an unabashed ass-kisser. The unspoken rule at Atlantic was that you never bothered Ahmet or Doug. If they wanted you, they'd find you. From the moment Toby started, he was constantly clamoring for their attention. As a result of all this, I resented Toby and never gave Doug his messages.

Toby appeared in my doorway.

"I'm busy, Toby." I looked behind him to see if Jason was on the way. The last thing I wanted was Toby to catch the scent of an embryonic deal.

"Do you mind if I shut the door?" Toby asked.

"Go ahead. But I only have a minute."

"I want to know why you're so rude to me. I mean, obviously you don't like me. Why?"

"OK, Toby—you want to know why? I'll tell you why. You're a fucking ass-kisser. I'm busting my ass to get into the A&R Department, and you just waltz in there with your family connections and you have the nerve to call me all day long like I'm your secretary. I take orders from Ahmet. He's earned it. You haven't."

"Listen, I like you and I want us to get along. Don't make it so impossible, OK?"

"Fine," I said. "I'll give you this: you have balls. I respect that."

Satisfied with our newly established détente, he left. I followed him into the hall and peered around for Jason. Still no sign of him.

I buzzed his office again.

"What are you doing that's so important up there, open-heart surgery?"

"Jesus, Dorothy. Keep your skirt on—I'll be right there."

When he finally arrived, I told him to close the door.

"Let me guess," he said, "you banged Bon Jovi last night."

"Better."

"Sambora too?"

I rolled my eyes. "No, smartass. I talked Jon into considering bringing Skid Row to Atlantic."

Jason and I huddled in my office, scheming. We needed a way to foul the Geffen deal and get Skid Row. First, I pumped Jason up, telling him that he needed this just as much as I did. Then we went to work on Tunc, who had once tried to sign Bon Jovi and kept the band's original demo tape in his desk drawer as a sort of talisman, a reminder of what could happen when you missed out on a new act. I told Tunc about the dinner at Bon Jovi's house and said we needed to rally as a company to fight Geffen. "Are we going to miss another multiplatinum act?" I asked him, almost as a taunt. I also suggested we get Ahmet involved.

Tunc promised he would speak to Ahmet, but I couldn't wait for that. When Ahmet arrived that afternoon, I burst into his office and said, "Ahmet, we need to sign Skid Row. They have the Bon Jovi tour."

"Tours don't sell records," he replied.

I knew he was wrong, but I wasn't going to challenge him. That would only turn him off. Undaunted, I went back to Tunc's office. "You have to go speak to him, Turk to Turk," I said to Tunc. "Aren't we tired of losing to Geffen? This will be huge, I promise. Tell him to fire me if it isn't."

Tunc called Ahmet, and I slunk back to my desk. It was agony. I had put Skid Row on the table, but Tunc and Ahmet excluded me from the most important conversation. I went to Jason's office to ease my nerves. "I don't want to be cut out of this," I said. "I don't want to be a secretary anymore."

Finally, Tunc buzzed me. "Honey, come in here," he said. I'd never been so happy to hear that gruff voice. I grabbed a pen and notepad and hurried into Ahmet's office. Ahmet was sitting in his usual place behind his desk, while Tunc paced the floor in front of him.

"Everybody wants this band," Tunc said. Then, turning to me: "Tell him."

"It's true," I said, weighing my words. "Everybody wants them, but Geffen is the most likely place for them to go." I knew that would needle him.

"Fuck Geffen," Ahmet said.

"You want Kalodner to get these guys?" Tunc pushed. "You want a fucking repeat of what happened with Bon Jovi? These guys are going to be a hit."

"Okay," Ahmet said. "We'll go see them."

I ordered a helicopter to take us to see Skid Row the next night in Allentown, Pennsylvania. The prospects were bleak—I had heard through the grapevine that Geffen was giving a shitload up front and a three-quarter mechanical rate. The mechanical rate is the percentage from each record sale that goes to the band. Geffen's offer was the standard industry rate, but Ahmet couldn't be counted on to match it, let alone beat it. Still, I couldn't back down now. As long as Ahmet got on the chopper, I knew we still had a chance.

On a freezing Saturday night in March 1988, I met Jason, Tunc, and a Turkish hanger-on who was rumored to be Ahmet's godson at the heliport on Thirty-Fourth Street. When Ahmet arrived, I could tell he was high. I asked his driver, Ray, what he was on. Ray was a tall African American man with a fun personality and one bad eye. Only Ahmet would hire a half-blind driver. Ray told me it was the usual mix—cocaine and vodka—but it made me nervous. I didn't want anything to go wrong, including Ahmet getting too fucked up to function.

As soon as we lifted off, Ahmet started drinking again. As for the rest of us, the mood was serious. Again, it was standard protocol to leave Ahmet alone unless he engaged you first, so we all sat silently in the helicopter like we were on our way to church.

Jenny had advised me to order two limos to pick us up at the heliport in Pennsylvania and told me to use Carey Limo, because Atlantic had an account with them. I followed her directions, figuring she had done this before, but I still felt nervous all the way there. When we landed, the limos were waiting, as arranged. I could breathe again.

"How was your trip?" Ahmet asked one of the drivers holding open a door.

"Fine, thanks. Just a little long," the driver said.

"Traffic?"

"No . . . we came from Pittsburgh."

Ahmet leveled me with a look. I knew something was wrong but I didn't know what. *They came on time, didn't they?* Once everyone had piled in the car, Ahmet turned to me. "You ordered the cars from Pittsburgh?" he screamed. "That's five hours away! This is going to cost me a fortune. You're fired, and I'm taking the money out of your last check." Not being well versed in Pennsylvania geography, I had trusted Jenny, and she had set me up. Ahmet berated me for most of the ride, and his elephant brain never forgot the incident. Even years later, he'd bring it up just to fuck with me.

He finished his tirade by calling me an idiot. I agreed. Then he got hungry. We drove around the small Pennsylvania town for twenty minutes, but the best place we could find was a twenty-four-hour International House of Pancakes. We ordered pancakes, bacon, waffles, and pitchers of soda and beer, and the bill came to fourteen dollars, which amused Ahmet to no end. He blew his nose with that kind of money.

Finally, we arrived at the club—it was actually a converted roller skating rink. Heavy metal music blasted from the sound system as we waited for the show to start. I felt nervous. I felt excited. Then I felt something else: Ahmet's hand between my legs. I tried to slap it away, but he was surprisingly strong for an old man. He moved up to my tits. I begged Tunc and the others to stop him, but they were too scared of him to help. He was like an octopus, eight arms flailing. I couldn't fucking believe it. I had taken my career into my own hands by bringing Ahmet here. My future rested on the outcome of this night. I was desperate to prove that I was more than a secretary—I knew I had the savvy to succeed as an executive. I wanted to be taken seriously, but Ahmet wasn't interested in my brain or my ears. He didn't see me as an asset to be developed. I was a piece of pussy in a packed nightclub, surrounded by cowards.

I don't know the laws in Pennsylvania, but in New York State, Ahmet's behavior qualified as sexual battery:

> Article 130, Class A Misdemeanor: A person is guilty of forcible touching when such a person intentionally, and for no legitimate purpose, forcibly touches the sexual or intimate parts of another person for the purpose of degrading or abusing such person; includes squeezing, grabbing, or pinching.

Again, however, it is worth noting that terms such as "sexual battery" weren't in anyone's vocabulary at the time. When you grow up in a world where men can grope you at whim and with impunity, you don't see it as something you have the power to stop. I also rationalized it—there was no guarantee I wouldn't get the same treatment at any other job. A woman could have her tits grabbed working at a bank just as easily as in the music industry. So I stuck with it. I still had my price, and every time they raised the stakes, I anted up.

I knew Ahmet didn't grab me out of sexual attraction. I could have been any girl; that's how high he was. Still I felt insulted, hurt, ashamed, and degraded. I also felt defiant. I was going to make this Skid Row deal happen no matter what. I'd show him and everyone else what I was worth.

Mercifully, Sebastian Bach took the stage, his long hair swinging, his gorgeous face puckered into a rocker's scowl, and Ahmet stopped groping me. Skid Row played the same forty-five-minute set I'd seen a month ago in New Jersey, but I was too nervous to enjoy it this time. I kept an eye constantly on Ahmet, trying to gauge his thoughts and feelings.

After the show, we went backstage and found ourselves with just the band—no girls, no hangers-on. Sebastian came right over to us, and I could tell from the way he looked at Ahmet that he was starstruck. Ahmet was an old pro at this; he knew just how to break through the awe. "Let's have a fucking drink, man!" he shouted. Everyone cheered. The Jack Daniel's came out and Ahmet started pounding, performing a feat of power drinking that seemed to impress the band more than his roster of platinum albums did. Then he trotted out his war stories— Mick Jagger, Robert Plant, Eric Clapton. Skid Row was in heaven. It was remarkable to witness a master hit maker working a room full of up-and-coming musicians. "You have that quality," he told Sebastian. I don't know who was happier to hear him say it—Sebastian or me.

When we boarded the helicopter an hour later Ahmet was wasted beyond repair. He kept grabbing at my legs. I'd had the foresight to wear shorts under my skirt. He pulled my legs apart and said, "She came prepared."

By the time we landed in Manhattan, it was four in the morning. Ahmet took one step on the tarmac and fell flat on his face. Ray scrambled to help him into the car. Looking at Ahmet sprawled out on the pavement, I didn't envy Ray's job. I did, however, understand it. Our first job at Atlantic was to protect Ahmet when he lost control. He was, after all, a living legend, not expendable like the rest of us.

As strange as it is to say of a man who sexually battered me, I still felt loyal to Ahmet. He had taken me in and shown me a world beyond my wildest fantasies. He had given me shelter, clothes, food, and perks that I could never have imagined growing up in Brooklyn. Where others saw my weaknesses as poison, Ahmet embraced them. Unlike my father, he accepted me and listened to me. My feelings for him were complex, and they still are. I lived in a "boys will be boys" world, where sexual harassment was taken for granted. I knew it was wrong, but I didn't consider fighting it. Fight it how, and with what power? The only option, it seemed, was to grit my teeth and bear it.

The physical effects of Ahmet's touching went away as soon as he took his hands off me. The mental and emotional effects were much more insidious. I began suffering from acute anxiety and panic attacks (though I didn't know what these conditions were at the time). The pressure was constant and unbearable. I took all the responsibility for Ahmet's actions on my shoulders, and it weighed me down.

———————

As usual with Ahmet, by the next morning all was forgotten. I told Noreen what had happened, and she blasted Tunc for his inaction, but Ahmet and I never spoke about it. When I came to work, Ahmet was already making calls from his home to Doug. He wanted to go after Skid Row. He called me and said, "Get me Doc McGhee." I quickly patched the call through. I wished I'd taken enough interest in the phones to figure out a way to eavesdrop on their conversation, but all I could do was go about my secretarial tasks, making Ahmet's appointments and taking his other calls, waiting to learn my fate.

On the off chance the deal went through, I felt terrified that they'd forget my role in it. I don't want to say everyone involved discounted me because I was Ahmet's secretary, but they didn't include me in any meetings. I had set the wheels in motion, but they had complete control over whether or not I got to take the ride.

After the phone call with Doc, Ahmet appeared in the office. I still didn't know anything. In desperation, I buzzed Jason.

"What's going on?"

"I'll call you back," he said.

Half an hour later, I saw Ahmet go into Tunc's office. I followed. "We got 'em!" Tunc said. Victory! I went around the room hugging and kissing Ahmet, Jason, and even nasty old Tunc. I felt confident and talented, maybe for the first time in my life.

A few weeks later, Ahmet called me into his office. I didn't suspect anything until I saw Doug there too. "You can go upstairs to the ninth floor," Doug said. "You've been promoted. I'm giving you a raise up to $30,000. Congratulations." Despite working so hard for this moment, I almost couldn't believe it. Forty years into its existence, Atlantic had just hired its first female A&R executive.

Me.

11

GOIN' DOWN

A&R HAD OFFICES ON THE ninth floor, but they didn't have an office for me. The floor was crammed and dirty, with barely enough space to walk among the balled-up paper and discarded trash. Jason kindly offered to share his office, so I brought in a desk and sat facing him. This worked in my favor—when he'd have important meetings, whether with Atlantic top brass, other A&R execs, or band managers, everyone in attendance couldn't help but notice me. It raised my profile in the A&R world and helped ease my transition from secretary to executive.

I decided to do something nice in return. I knew that Jason loved Aerosmith, so for his birthday, I asked Tim Collins to have Steven Tyler call him and wish him a happy birthday. I also bought him a platinum Aerosmith album with his name on it, paid for out of my own pocket. We were thick as thieves.

Doug ruled over A&R like a high school principal. We had to arrive at 9:30 AM and sign our names on a sheet. The sheet went to Doug's office at 9:40, no matter what. If you came in late, he'd call you to his office for a personal reprimand. Perhaps that sounds like a light sentence, but keep in mind the power Doug had over us all. We craved his approval and cringed at his criticism. He was parent, teacher, and guru all in one.

I had no problem being punctual. Every day, I woke up excited to go to work. Nothing had ever seemed so meaningful. I had my dream job and worked three feet away from my best friend. I had money rolling in and a promising new project to jump-start my career. Ahmet must have sensed my happiness getting out of hand.

Before my promotion I had been working on Atlantic's fortieth-anniversary celebration. We scheduled a concert at Madison Square Garden for May 14, 1988, complete with performances by Led Zeppelin, Phil Collins, Foreigner, Crosby, Stills & Nash, the Bee Gees, Yes, Wilson Pickett, the Coasters, Average White Band, the Manhattan Transfer, Laura Branigan, Genesis, the Rascals, Roberta Flack, and Ben E. King, among others. The show was going to be broadcast live on FM radio and on HBO.

I played an important role in the planning, but not an irreplaceable one, so it came as a surprise when Ahmet called me to his office and said, "I need you back. You know all the people, and I don't have time to explain it to someone else." Ahmet ordered me to report to my old desk the following morning. He had demoted me. I was his secretary again, my A&R career seemingly over before it had even started.

The next day, I showed up in a rage. I ordered Doug's coffee like I had so many times before, and when he came to pick it up I tried to confront him. Before I could get a word out, he put his hands up and said, "Uh, uh, uh." He pointed at Ahmet's office: "He's the boss. You have to do what he says. It's not up to me." But as an A&R executive, I reported to Doug, not Ahmet. I couldn't believe he'd throw me under the bus like that. I was humiliated. My old friends and acquaintances looked at me with surprise and asked what I was doing back on the second floor. *That's a good question*, I thought. I knew they wouldn't pull this crap on a man.

Jenny handled the backstage passes for the fortieth-anniversary show, and whatever affinity she had once felt for me must have evaporated for good, because she didn't give me a pass. I didn't feel too bad about it. She also didn't give passes to the department heads. It was the limousine fiasco all over again—Jenny on another power trip.

Walking around the Garden during the show, I ran into the executive producer. "Why aren't you backstage?" he said, shocked. I told him I didn't have a pass, and he produced an all-access laminate. Sometimes small acts of kindness make the most impact. It felt good that someone had the heart and guts to look out for me. With the laminate around my neck, I went backstage and saw Ahmet lying on a bed like King Tut in the middle of a room full of rock stars. This was rock 'n' roll heaven—Mick Jagger, Robert Plant, Jimmy Page, Paul Stanley, Bob Geldof. Even Kalodner was there, despite being Ahmet's enemy and working for Atlantic's rival. I made sure Jenny saw me. The look on her face was revenge enough.

After the party, I assumed Ahmet would send me back to the ninth floor so I could finally start my A&R career. Ahmet never even mentioned it. When I brought it up, he said he wouldn't let me go until he found a replacement secretary. Naturally he hated everyone he interviewed. Our relationship became strained.

"You're being unfair," I told him.

"I don't care," he shot back. "You're here for as long as I need you."

Fine, I thought. *If Ahmet wants to play it that way, then game on.* I became cold to him and cut out all banter. He could make me do a secretary's work again, but I wanted him to know he couldn't make me *be* his secretary again.

I was demoted for two months of awful anxiety, performing two jobs—secretary and A&R rep. Even after Ahmet found a new secretary, I had to train her, which meant more waiting. When he finally let me go back upstairs, I had been gone almost three months. I felt I had no choice but to put up with this shit or lose my job. Doug had already made it clear he wouldn't stand up for me. I felt the powerlessness I always feared, and it was horrible. After taking such pains all my life to make sure I never owed a man anything, I found myself in a position where men controlled me almost completely. I felt like a yo-yo, up and down, up and down. One minute they liked me, my career was moving forward, and I felt supported and valuable. The next minute they spurned me, my career stalled, and I felt worthless. It was a sickening ride.

I went back to the ninth floor with a vengeance and demanded my own office. Jason helped, persuading Doug to visit us on nine. Doug almost never left his cushy lair on the second floor, so when he stepped out of the elevator, it was like President Carter touring the South Bronx. Disgust showed on his face as he surveyed the carnage.

He found the head of A&R, Richard Steinberg, napping in his office. He slammed the door, startling Richard awake. Doug took one look at Jason's office stuffed with two desks and said, "No way." He pointed at a tiny office across the hall that belonged to Richard's secretary, Angie.

"Put her out in the pit with the other secretaries," Doug said. "Dorothy will take Angie's office."

Facilities came and moved everything that day. I felt free at last. I knew they'd never put a man through what I had just gone through, but I was just happy to start my work in A&R. I'd been humiliated, screwed over, forgotten, taken for granted, and even abused, but they couldn't stop me. I survived.

12

DAMNED IF YOU DO

DESPITE THE MYTHOLOGICAL NOTION OF A&R people stumbling on some unknown act at a nightclub, that wasn't how it happened when I started my career. There were no more Bob Dylans breathing out their brilliant songs in dimly lit cafes, and no one in the music industry wasted time trolling around the Village looking for someone like him. It was never blind luck—although we did have a saying about A&R: "Even a blind pig finds an acorn every once in a while." Rather, we'd get tips about bands through people we knew, and go see them at specially arranged shows. The hot clubs in New York at the time were the Cat Club, CBGB, the Ritz, and Kenny's Castaways.

Sometimes we'd also travel to the West Coast. In August 1988 Jason and I went to Los Angeles on my first trip as an executive. When traveling for business, Doug required us to write a memo stating the purpose of the trip and how long we'd be gone. After reading my memo, Doug told Jason to take me to the Ivy restaurant, one of L.A.'s most exclusive spots. Maybe he felt bad about my demotion and was trying to make it up to me. I appreciated the kindness.

Jason and I flew out together and stayed in separate rooms at the Beverly Hills Hotel. When I got to my room, I found a bouquet of flowers with a note that read: "Welcome to L.A. Love, John." Kalodner was in London; I was free to do as I pleased.

The next day, as I prepared to visit Atlantic's West Coast offices and meet with our bands and managers there, Jason gave me my first lesson in the life of a traveling A&R executive. We didn't work in an office; we conducted our meetings by the pool. Doug didn't exactly condone this behavior, but we had all calls transferred to the pool, so he couldn't figure out where we were.

After our poolside meetings, we often went to Melrose Avenue and shopped at Fred Segel's for the latest fashion befitting a hip A&R person. Evenings we ate at the Palm, the Ivy, and Morton's. We spent our nights going to clubs and hanging out with managers of the biggest bands in the business—Alan Niven (Great White, Guns N' Roses), Glen Parrish (Stevie Nicks), Brian Avnet (the Manhattan Transfer), Tom Miller (Manowar), Michael and Terry Lippman (George Michael). I also hung with Tim Collins, Aerosmith's manager and Kalodner's friend, this time as an equal. Jason and I watched Tori Amos and Joe Chiccarelli in the recording studio and made frequent trips to see record producer Keith Olsen at his studio, Goodnight L.A., in the valley. Olsen was and is a legend, with thirty-nine gold, twenty-four platinum, and twelve multi-platinum records to his name. We spent hours watching him record Fiona's album. It was the fucking life.

We were officially in L.A. to watch Skid Row participate in the annual T. J. Martell Foundation sports weekend for charity. Doc McGhee had flown the band out for the event for a little PR as they prepared to record their first album. Doc was short and bald, and he was the funniest manager I ever knew. We used to call him "P. T. Barnum," the greatest showman on earth. Mötley Crüe made him famous as "Dr. Feelgood" from the eponymous album and single. Yes, Doc McGhee was a drug dealer who had just pleaded guilty to smuggling forty thousand pounds of marijuana out of South America. You read that number right. *Forty. Thousand.*

Jason and I thought we'd be spending time with Doc, but instead we got his younger brother, Scott. Scott was a former football player with the Chicago Bears whose career was cut short due to injury. Tall and good looking—the opposite of Doc in many ways—Scott was just as fun as his brother was to be around. He didn't have Doc's street smarts, but Doc made him Skid Row's new manager, so we dealt with him.

Jason and I met Scott and the members of Skid Row for a quick bite at R.J.'s for Ribs in Beverly Hills. After dinner, we had plans to catch a concert at the Rainbow Bar & Grill on Sunset Boulevard. As we ate, I noticed a group of girls celebrating a Sweet Sixteen birthday. So did Sebastian Bach. Sebastian (or "Miss Texas," as Kalodner called him because he was so pretty) began teasing the girls. The girls' parents didn't find it funny, and we had to make a mad dash out of the restaurant before the cops came.

That's when it hit me—I was barely older than these boys, but I was in charge of them. My hopes and dreams rested on their wild, mischievous backs. Doc had once explained bands like Skid Row to me, and his words came back to me as a warning: "Ninety percent of these guys are uneducated. You take them and put them on a stage, they wave in one direction, then twenty thousand people wave back. They feel their power. Next, they want only the red M&M's, no brown ones. Their bad behavior is enabled constantly by those around them." I didn't have to look far to see it happening in real time. Jason seemed to love everything Miss Texas did—like most A&R people, he wanted to live the rock star lifestyle, but he had to settle for watching from the sidelines. As for me, I worried about keeping these children in line long enough to record an album and solidify my career.

We left the Rainbow around 2:00 AM, and Jason and I drove back to the hotel. As I got ready for bed, I heard a knock on my door. I answered it in panties and a *Kick* T-shirt. It was Scott McGhee.

"What the fuck are you doing here?" I said.

"It's already so late, and I'm too drunk to go to Doc's. Please, can I stay here?"

I considered it for a moment. We had a tee time at the T. J. Martell event in six hours.

"OK," I said, "but let's just be clear, I am not going to fuck you. Got it?"

He nodded.

"There's the love seat," I said. Scott couldn't possibly fit on the love seat. He was too tall. He gave me a dumb look.

"OK," I said. "Just get in the bed and go to sleep. I'm beat."

He whipped off his pants so fast he almost tripped on them. As he stood in his underwear I noticed he had the body of a professional athlete—built, chiseled, and muscular. He jumped into bed and said goodnight. I rolled over and began nodding off. I jolted awake when I felt Scott's dick against my lower back.

"Take your dick off my back and go to sleep, or I'll snap it off."

He did. A few hours later I awoke in Scott's long, muscular arms. I had to admit it felt nice, but I knew it wouldn't be worth the trouble. I slid out of his arms and jumped into the shower. I ordered us both breakfast and aspirin because I knew he would be hungover. When the trays arrived, I woke him up and threw him a robe. He quickly showered and came out to eat. He drank his coffee, took his aspirin, and said, "This is nice. It's like being married. No sex, but a good meal."

I learned an important lesson from my night with Scott McGhee: don't let a man in your hotel room unless you plan to bang him. It sends a mixed message, and you'll pay for it in the end. After that night, Scott never treated me the same. He began cutting me out of everything involving Skid Row. He didn't understand that I had rejected not Scott the man, but Scott the manager. I was trying to be taken seriously by Jason, Doc, Bon Jovi, and Skid Row. I felt crushing pressure to deliver, and I didn't intend to fuck it up by sleeping with the band's manager.

It was a lonely position. I couldn't really talk to anyone about it. Even my best friend, as a man, couldn't understand the double standards I faced, or the constant, grinding slog every day to simply earn respect. I had no female friends to commiserate with. None of the wives or girlfriends attached to the music business liked me. To women, I was just another chick to keep a wary eye on. To men, I was just another piece of flesh to make a pass at. With Scott, I found myself caught in the classic trap—damned if you do and damned if you don't.

When we got to the golf course, Doc put his arm around me and said, "Did that maggot hurt you?"

"No," I said.

"Did he touch you?"

"We only slept together," I said. It came out all wrong.

"I bet he was all over you like a cheap suit."

"No, Doc. I'm sorry you're upset," I said.

Everyone lined up on the tee box to take a swing—Doc put up $25,000 for the first person to get a hole in one. He also strategically placed models in bikinis who took their tops off as the men tried to swing. Classic Doc.

———————

Back in New York, I thought about everything Jason had done not just for me, but also for the company. With Skid Row and White Lion, he became the only executive at Atlantic signing rock hits. In fact, other than Larry in the Dance Department, Jason was the only executive signing hits at all. I had just watched him work in L.A., and I saw the dedication he showed his artists. He made only $50,000—far less than people who brought in little to nothing, including the head of A&R, Richard Steinberg. Jason deserved more, so I took a play out of Doug's book to help him get it.

Whenever Doug's contract came up, he'd have Irving Azoff, the chairman of MCA Records, come to Atlantic. They'd walk around the building, making it look like Irving had come to offer Doug a job. Doug used that as leverage to get more money at Atlantic. Working on the same principle, I asked Kalodner to set up an interview for Jason with David Geffen.

At that time, Geffen had a penthouse apartment across from Central Park on East Sixtieth Street. He agreed to meet Jason there the next time he visited New York. For Geffen at least, the meeting was more than theater. He offered Jason a job. Jason turned it down, saying Atlantic was his family, and he could never leave. Geffen's response: "You're stupid. I'll never offer you a job again."

Jason returned from the meeting looking worn out and beat up. Apparently, in addition to calling him stupid, Geffen also said something about Jason's physical appearance, something Jason found insulting and embarrassing. He wouldn't even tell me what Geffen said, but I could tell he was hurt. The best I could guess was that Geffen told Jason to get a nose job.

Maybe Jason came away from the meeting with a few scars, but after Geffen's offer, Doug promoted Jason to vice president and department head of A&R. Jason got a raise and took another major step up the corporate ladder. I celebrated the promotion as much as Jason did, not knowing that I had just put in motion the end of our friendship and the end of my career at Atlantic.

Damned if you do.

13

HOWDY, PARTNER

AHMET HAD JUST FORMED A country music division in Nashville, and he wanted to go check it out. He invited me to join his posse. I had partied with Ahmet before, but I had never partied with Ahmet on the road. There was a difference. It seemed impossible, but he had levels of debauchery I hadn't yet seen.

I met Ahmet and company—including Janice—at Butler Aviation, a private airport attached to LaGuardia, where Warner kept its corporate planes. Every executive dreamed of flying on these planes, but to me they seemed cramped and small. We arrived in Nashville quickly and found cars waiting to take us to the Atlantic offices. There, I met Rick Blackburn, president of Atlantic Records in Nashville. Rick looked like a cowboy, and he acted like one too. He was famous as the man who dropped Johnny Cash from Columbia Records in 1986. I could tell Ahmet didn't like him.

Ahmet started giving his typical crowd-warming speech, the one he usually gave to break the ice, but Rick cut him off. He launched into some bullshit lecture about how great it was to live in Nashville. He bragged about his huge ranch with acres of land and horses. He bragged about his Porsche. He bragged that he didn't have to pay state income tax. He didn't notice Ahmet's face during this ill-advised speech, but I did. I knew what was coming. When Rick finally stopped speaking,

Ahmet said, "I'm paying you too much money." Ahmet looked at me and said, "Right?"

"I don't have a Porsche," I blurted out.

Rick gave me a dirty look. Obviously Rick didn't know who he worked for. Ahmet was a man of wealth and taste—homes in New York, Southampton, Paris, Turkey; a vast art collection; a Swiss bank account. The last thing Ahmet would do was worry about state taxes. Strike that—the *last* thing Ahmet would do was pick up horseshit on some farm in Tennessee like a fucking peasant. *Off to a bad start, Rick.*

We went to eat at some barbecue joint and by the time we finished Ahmet was stinking drunk. "Let's go to the strip club!" he shouted. Ahmet knew I had never been to a strip club and he wanted to fill that void in my life. His favorite club in Nashville was called 50 Beautiful Girls and 1 Ugly One, and it must have been good, because it was packed on a weeknight.

The club was on Demonbreun Street, now a hot neighborhood in Nashville and the home of many record companies. We weren't there long before Ahmet decided I needed a lap dance. Before I knew what was happening, one of the girls thrust her tits in my face. *What a way to make a living*, I thought, and I didn't mean the stripper. As the lap dance continued, I noticed a lecherous twinkle in Ahmet's eye. I could read his mind—he wanted to see if I would kiss a girl, because if I did, I might be into trying a threesome. Ahmet never met a threesome he didn't love. Most men I knew in the business were the same way. Sometimes it seemed like we only talked about threesomes. I had certainly become more adventurous sexually, but the notion of sharing my bed with another girl didn't appeal to me. I made sure the guys at the office knew it, and they teased me relentlessly, calling me a prude, asking how could I possibly make a judgment call like that without at least trying it. I knew where this evening would go with Ahmet if I didn't stop it.

"Nothing's happening!" I yelled at Ahmet.

We stayed at 50 Pretty Girls and 1 Ugly one until 2:00 AM. We would have stayed longer, but that's when they stopped serving booze in Nashville. Ahmet tried to pressure Rick into driving to Kentucky to buy liquor, but Janice convinced him to let it go. We all went back to the Loews Vanderbilt, the best hotel in Nashville, and as I walked to my room, I saw Ahmet passed out on the floor in the hallway.

Sometimes I hated Ahmet for making our relationship so fucked up, and in that moment, the hatred welled up inside me. I couldn't help myself; I kicked him. That was my revenge. When I dragged my ass downstairs a few hours later, there was Ahmet, dressed and ready to go, looking fresh as a fucking daisy. I don't know how he did it. Maybe that was his revenge.

On the flight back to New York, I caught a rare glimpse of Ahmet's compassionate side. We hit some turbulence and he could tell I was afraid, so he made me sit in the copilot's chair and stood behind me saying, "See, see, there's nothing out there but blue sky." I tried to get up. "No," he said, "face your fears." It worked. I have never been afraid to fly since.

The trip to Nashville was the first of many I took with Ahmet as an A&R executive. I soon became a connoisseur of strip clubs around the country. Some of the best included:

- The Gold Club in Atlanta, Georgia: Ahmet's favorite dancer at the Gold Club was an older woman who looked like the female Tasmanian Devil. All she needed was lipstick and a bow. She came out in a one-piece bathing suit and he went crazy. I found out later from the manager that she was one of the club's best earners. I didn't believe him. "How can that be?" I asked. He said: "You have no idea how sick men are." That was an important lesson. All women are beautiful. It doesn't matter what we've been told by beauty magazines. Any woman with any body can turn on a guy somewhere.
- Rick's Cabaret in Houston, Texas: One night I went to Rick's Cabaret with Skid Row and Doc and Scott McGhee. It was brutally hot. The guys in Skid Row were all in their early twenties, and it was like they'd never seen tits before. They didn't tip well, either. The place was fantastic, though. The girls danced so fast up and down

the pole you had to wonder how they did it. They were athletes. I envied them in a way, because they were free with their bodies, and they had power over men.

- Pure Platinum in Fort Lauderdale, Florida: Another Skid Row experience. They were animals, running and jumping all over everything. It was like preschool. We were in the VIP section and we had money, so if anybody got into trouble, we'd just pay off the management and the girls.

Eventually, I got used to traveling the Ahmet Ertegun way. I got used to phone calls at three o'clock in the morning, and hearing that raspy croak say, "What are you doing?" *What am I doing? I'm fucking sleeping.* I got used to his orders: "Get me a vodka. Get me a stripper. Get me a hooker." I got used to his reprimands when I'd say, "Where am I supposed to get a stripper at 3 AM, Ahmet?" He'd answer: "I don't know, get a *Screw* magazine. You're fucking useless."

I still had access to his Rolodex, and I'd go through it calling his caravan of loose women to meet him wherever he was going. Soon I had guys of my own dotted across the map. Of course, I was one of the few single people in this debauched scene, but God forbid any of us control our sexual urges. I imitated the men around me, especially Ahmet, still not understanding that I couldn't live the way they did. I didn't have the money, or power, or fame. I'd learn that soon enough.

14

MAGIC MIKE

As the summer of 1988 ended I went to Lake Geneva, Wisconsin, to watch Skid Row record their debut album. I had never been to Wisconsin before, and it was a jarring change from Manhattan—nothing but trees and sky. I remember hoping aliens would beam me up and drop me somewhere exciting.

Returning from a walk one afternoon, I saw a large tour bus pull into the hotel parking lot. *Finally, some action.* I figured I might know someone on the bus, and even if not, it would be exciting to see someone from the music business. I walked toward the bus and saw Michael Hutchence. I ran to him and gave him a big hug and kiss, and we walked into the lobby together. He asked for my room number and said he would come by to hang out in an hour. *Hang out?* My head spun with the possibilities. I went back to my room and waited for him. Soon, I heard a knock on the door.

If I had to conjure the quintessential rock star, it would be the man I saw when I opened my hotel-room door. He was tall, with long arms and fingers, full lips, and flowing hair. You could tell this guy got pussy for miles.

"Do you want something to drink?" I asked.

He asked for a beer. Luckily, I had stashed a few beers in the minibar for when the guys from Skid Row came to the room—they were like a bunch of college frat boys looking to get drunk and laid all the time.

I told Michael we were recording their debut record, and that even Jon Bon Jovi was there helping out. We sat on the bed discussing how everything was going with the *Kick* tour, but we both knew he hadn't come for chitchat. As I got up from the bed to put my drink on the dresser, he followed me and backed me up against the wall. He lowered his head to kiss me. His lips were bigger than mine, and I felt a rush of chemicals take over my body. The feeling I got from him was like a drug.

After he kissed me, I took off his glasses and placed them gently on the dresser. Our brown eyes met, and he gave me the warmest smile. My heart melted on the spot. He pressed against me and lifted my skirt, pulling off my panties. I unbuckled his belt, pulled his pants down, and wrapped my legs around him like a monkey climbing a tree.

We banged all over the room. We went through the first eight positions of the Kama Sutra like it was nothing, and yet I couldn't get out of my own head. I knew that rock stars dated models. I wasn't Miss Denmark; I wasn't even Miss Brooklyn. I had also heard artists complain that the models were wooden and rigid in bed. How would I compare? On top of that, I thought of Ahmet. After all, Michael was one of his artists. I felt that Ahmet's reputation hinged on if I was any good. I also wanted to be asked back for a repeat performance.

Michael didn't seem preoccupied at all. He carried me to the window and pushed me into the venetian blinds. They fell to the floor with a crash. I was laughing but still trying to focus. I must have been making too much noise, and he put his hand over my mouth, only turning me on more.

My previous sexual experiences didn't compare to sex with Michael. It was like I'd been driving around in a run-down Ford Pinto my whole life, and all of a sudden I jumped in a Ferrari and went from zero to 150. I understood why the man got applause onstage and off. I had never experienced such complete attention to detail. He touched every part of me, asking at each step if I liked it. Most men I had encountered could think only of their own pleasure. He even remarked on my pedicure and said that my toes were perfectly proportioned from large to small in the proper order.

Finally we hit the bed, exhausted. His mane of hair lay splayed out next to me—I almost thought I was lying next to a girl. *Damn!* I thought.

This is what sex is supposed to be like. I've been doing it wrong all these years. Michael whipped out his cigarettes, took a puff, and said to me, "You are beautiful." No one had ever called me beautiful before, but I suppose that's what made Michael such a great musician. He was a poet, and he made his living with words. He knew it was far more intoxicating to call me beautiful than pretty.

"The same could be said of you," I said.

He invited me to his show that night and said that after the show we should definitely see each other. I was spaced out at that point, just nodding and agreeing to everything.

He got up to take a shower and took a look around the room. "Jesus Christ, I'll certainly pay for all of this," he said. He really was a gentleman. "No, this is on Atlantic Records," I said, proud that I had the power of the expense account. Then, I imagined how it would look on the report: Venetian Blinds—Lake Geneva, Wisconsin—$32—For INXS. I was sure Ahmet would approve that.

15

FRACTURES

"How was the trip?"

After returning from Wisconsin I stopped by Ahmet's office to catch up. Though I answered to Doug now, Ahmet remained my confidant, my role model, and my adviser. I sat down across from him and said, "You're not going to believe this."

He leaned back in his chair, put his glasses on his head, and said, "Tell me."

"I fucked Michael Hutchence."

Ahmet practically slobbered as I gave him the inside story, the one I entrusted to only a few intimate friends. If I were being true to myself, I would have admitted that I knew it was wrong to bang an artist, especially Hutch. INXS was Doug Morris's act, which meant Michael was technically my boss's employee. Besides, at Atlantic, the right to bang artists was reserved for titles—president and up.

I tried to rationalize it away. *I'm not Michael's A&R person*, I thought. *I have nothing to do with his career*. Ultimately, though, it was Ahmet's gleeful approbation of my story that allowed the guilt to subside. If the king says it's OK, how can a peasant disagree?

"I hope you didn't embarrass me," Ahmet said. I didn't tell him that I had the same thought midbanging. I did tell him that we wrecked the hotel room and that I put it on the expenses. Ahmet barely registered surprise. As I got up to leave, Ahmet looked at me with pride.

"You did good," he said.

Michael showed me the mountaintop. Throughout the autumn and winter of 1988, it seemed all the men in my life decided to show me the valley. Perhaps fittingly, Ahmet kicked off my descent.

Skid Row had a gig at the Cat Club in the East Village to stay limber while waiting for their album release and subsequent tour. I took Ahmet to see them as a victory lap. I felt proud of my role in signing the band and wanted to get him excited about the project. He arrived with Atlantic's cleaning lady—an age-appropriate date for once. He was drunk and high, as usual, but I didn't feel nervous this time. The last time I took Ahmet to see Skid Row, I was a secretary. This time, I was an *executive*.

I sat with Ahmet and the cleaning woman at a table in the corner. After a few songs, I realized something was wrong with the band. Sebastian could barely squawk out the notes, the guitars jangled out of tune, and the audience went limp. Ahmet grabbed my hand and squeezed until it hurt. Then he squeezed harder, his temper winding tighter and tighter like a guitar string about to snap. The band couldn't get it together, and Ahmet squeezed harder still, cocaine and booze fueling his rage. I was scared. He clenched my hand like a vise. Just before I thought my bones would break, Ahmet decided he'd seen enough.

He lifted my arm and slammed it on the table.

"This," he growled, "is what you made me spend my fucking money on?"

I was stunned. Never in my life had I experienced anything like it. My parents never even spanked me as a child. Pain shot up and down my arm. Shock numbed the pain. I wanted to escape, afraid he'd hurt me again, but I had nowhere to go. When the show ended, Ahmet and I went backstage. I took refuge by Skid Row's guitarist, Dave "the Snake" Sabo. He must have felt my fear. "What happened?" he asked. I brushed him off, slipped out of the dressing room, and went home. That night, shame and guilt took turns tying knots in my stomach. I knew Ahmet was wrong to have hurt me, but I believed it was my fault. *How could I have let Ahmet down like that? What if he fires me?*

The next day bruises covered my swollen arm, so I went to the doctor. He took X-rays and found a hairline fracture in my forearm. He asked how it happened. "My boss did it," I said. "He didn't mean it." The doctor, recognizing those infamous words—"He didn't mean it"—tried to help me. He explained that I had experienced abuse and told me my options. I laughed it off. *Abuse? Me? No, this was just part of my job.*

I really believed it was OK. It was my fault. It was the band's fault. It was anyone's fault but Ahmet's. I enabled his behavior, just like everyone else around him. That's how the legend of Ahmet Ertegun continued. He could fracture his A&R executive's arm and walk away without consequences. No one wanted to stop the gravy train from rolling, so no one stood up to him—not me, not the artists, not the managers, not Tunc, not Sheldon, not even Doug. A few days later, during a conversation with Doug, I brought up the incident, and he said, "What do you want me to do about it?" I knew that no one at the company would protect me. Instead of making a scene, I wore long sleeves until the bruises went away. Again, I rationalized it. *Life is all about compromise. We all have to pay a price for what we want.* I wanted to be an A&R executive, and this was the price I had to pay.

So I thought.

Next, I ran afoul of Doug. Michele Anthony, the executive vice president of Sony Music (and Tommy Mottola's right-hand woman), lived in the same building as John Kalodner in L.A. I met her through John, and she and I became close. When Sony wanted to poach me for their A&R Division, Michele invited me to lunch and asked if I would take a meeting with Tommy Mottola. I didn't want to leave Atlantic, but I wasn't an idiot. Mottola was one of the biggest names in the business. I took the meeting.

Sony Records had headquarters just across the street from Rockefeller Center, so I didn't make a big deal about it. No one even knew why I left for an hour in the middle of the day, and most likely no one cared. Tommy had a huge office on a high floor in the CBS building. He showed me his vast guitar collection, including one signed by Bruce Springsteen. I had never met Tommy before, but I felt like I knew him. He reminded me of my brother, with his penchant for projecting that Italian mafioso image. I knew a bit about his background already. I knew he was friends with John "Sonny" Franzese (from the Colombo crime family), who was a silent partner in Buddah Records. I also knew he was friends with Louis Gigante, a Catholic priest whose brother was Vinny "the Chin" Gigante, godfather of the Genovese crime family.

The meeting went well, and Tommy said he wanted me to meet Donnie Ienner, president of Columbia Records. He suggested we do it during Grammy week in Los Angeles. I thanked him for his time, left the CBS building, walked across the street, and went back to my office. Before I could sit down, Doug called me into his office. I'd barely stepped in his door when he laid into me. "You just met with Tommy Mottola?" he screamed. "How could you do such a thing? You're disloyal." I understood in a flash how connected the men in the music business were. Mottola must have called Doug right after I left and told him about our meeting. There was no other way Doug could have known so soon. I was sure Mottola did it just to fuck with Doug. These guys had the mentality of children arguing over who gets to rule the fort.

Now in a defensive position, one I was becoming used to with Doug, I pled my case. "I don't want to leave Atlantic," I said, "but it's Tommy Mottola calling. What was I supposed to do, pass up a meeting with him?"

"Yes," Doug said. "And I'd better not hear of you being disloyal to me again."

Lesson learned: there are no secrets in the music business. I left Doug's office reeling. Of course, I didn't mention Doug's games with Irving Azoff, or how he reamed me out for something he regularly did, or how Jason had just done the same thing and Doug had given him a raise and a promotion.

I realized how much Doug and Ahmet had in common. On the outside they seemed so different, but deep down, both men expected total loyalty, and both would explode with shock when they didn't get it. I already expected this behavior from Ahmet. The more I got to know Doug, the more I expected it from him. I did not, however, expect it from my best friend.

After leaving Doug's office, I ran into Jason, and he started yelling about disloyalty. I could barely take him seriously. This was even more ridiculous than what I had just heard from Doug. Jason apparently didn't remember the meeting I had set up for him with David Geffen, or how that had led to his current salary and title.

In fact, since his promotion, I could feel Jason starting to turn on me. It was like watching a living, breathing example of the age-old principle that power corrupts. Jason hired new assistants, including Wendy

Berry from Def Jam, whom he eventually married, and he ordered an expensive new desk and office furniture. He idolized Doug and began dressing in cheap suits like him. Even his vocabulary changed. He started using SAT words, putting on bullshit airs of scholarly refinement. I didn't know him anymore.

Then he started hiring friends to work in the A&R Department, and he automatically paid them more than me. He told me about it, too—he'd say that these guys were lawyers and businessmen and they expected a certain salary. Never mind that they had no experience in A&R; they were men.

It is a horrible, powerless feeling to watch a friendship disintegrate. Jason was my boss now. Neither of us knew how to adapt to that. He fluctuated, sometimes treating me like his best friend, sometimes treating me like a piece of property, like Ahmet did. He'd go from the old Jason, laughing and joking, to the boss Jason, barking out orders as though I were a useless subordinate, and he'd change so fast I couldn't keep up. We had been too close for too long to adjust to this change. After a while, I no longer knew where I stood. Jason, my only refuge from the constant up-and-down yo-yo of emotions that Ahmet and Doug put me through, now had the yo-yo tied to his finger.

I wanted to escape, to distance myself from everything that had let me down. When I started working at Atlantic, I believed it would satisfy the need I'd always felt to prove my worth. It didn't. Even as an executive, I still felt powerless, taken for granted, and denied. My family didn't help—after my raise they started asking for money. Worse, I now earned more than my father, and it made me feel guilty, as if I had broken some unwritten law. Even New York seemed to have turned on me: the subway was shitty, the city was dirty, and I had no friends.

Coincidentally, an opening for director of A&R had just come up in Atlantic's West Coast Division. I loved Los Angeles. In L.A. the sun was always shining. In L.A. I woke up every day thinking, *Isn't it great to be alive?* In L.A. I had a great group of friends and professional acquaintances who respected me as an executive. I'll never forget going to see Tori Amos record at producer Richard Landis's gorgeous house on Mullholland Drive and gasping at the vista of the city below—all palm trees and sunlight and swimming pools in every backyard. This was my escape. I asked Jason to consider me for the job, and he laughed in my face. "You're not director material," he said. "Plus you'd be the only A&R person out there. You're not capable."

If Ahmet or Doug had said that to me, I might have believed it. Coming from Jason it rang hollow. *Not capable?* I outranked him in education. I had more business savvy than he did (he might've been happy to stay in the same job at the same salary forever if I hadn't helped him get a raise and a title). Plus, I knew the guys on the West Coast—I couldn't have done worse than they did.

That's when I knew our problems went beyond a crumbling friendship. Jason didn't respect me anymore. He began treating me the way all the other men did, like I was an expendable little nothing, not worth the trouble of taking seriously. I don't know how or why it happened. I want to believe that it was corporate culture's fault. He had been promoted to a world where women did not belong, where a man could feel his power and wield it without consequence. I want to believe that as Jason felt this power pumping into him, he realized the difference between us. Given that I was a female of lower rank, my attempts to maintain our friendship threatened his power because being someone's best friend is an admission of equality. By the rules of his new world, he had to put me in my place. Maybe I'm being too kind to Jason. Maybe the disrespect was within him all along and had nothing to do with his promotion. Whatever the case, I didn't intend to put up with it.

In all, it had been a year of painful transitions. Yet I counted 1988 as one of the best years of my life, both because of Jason, Doug, Kalodner, and Ahmet and in spite of them. I was living my dream, and in most ways the reality lived up to the fantasy. After only a year and a half in the music business, I had helped sign a promising new band, become an executive, and watched that band record its debut album. I had held my own with businessmen and rock stars, both in the conference room and in the bedroom, and I counted some of the industry's elite figures as close friends.

I remembered Sister Rose Ellen's warning: "Men are going to try to break you." They had tried. Some even tried literally (my fractured forearm had healed, no thanks to Ahmet). Only I didn't break. I kept rising.

16

PLATINUM

SKID ROW'S SELF-TITLED DEBUT CAME out on January 24, 1989. On the backs of three singles—"Youth Gone Wild," "18 and Life," and "I Remember You"—the album hit number six on the *Billboard* Hot 200 chart. MTV put the music videos in heavy rotation, and *Skid Row* eventually sold more than five million copies. It was the bestselling album of the year for WEA.

Not bad for a first shot.

I loved the vindication of success. Doug loved the money pouring in (later that year, Doug gave Jason a $20,000 bonus, and I got $1,500). I continued to prove my worth, helping to orchestrate meetings for Doug and Ahmet with Tim Collins and Alan Niven, the managers of Aerosmith and Guns N' Roses, respectively. After these meetings, Doug gave me a raise to $50,000.

The raise felt good. I still yearned for Doug's approval, and money was the ultimate approval in this business. The greatest feeling of all, however, was turning on the radio and hearing a song I helped discover blaring from the speakers. The first time I heard "Youth Gone Wild" coming over the airwaves, I felt like I had cured cancer.

All of a sudden, I was in high demand. I began traveling the country to mingle with the elites of the music industry. On January 26, Jason and I flew to Dallas for the opening of the Bon Jovi/Skid Row tour. The dark clouds over our relationship briefly lifted, and we felt giddy as kids as we chased the band both of us had worked so hard to sign.

Normally, A&R people didn't get to travel with a tour outside of New York City, but Doug made a special allowance for us. That was another part of Doug's style: he didn't micromanage. He let us out on a long leash and only pulled it in when we fucked up.

In Dallas, we stayed at the Four Seasons Hotel alongside Doc McGhee and the band. Hanging with Ahmet had already given me a taste of the finer things—private jets, high-end hotels, and luxurious spas—but those perks had nothing to do with me. They were functions of my proximity to Ahmet. Now, I had earned them.

———

Skid Row's success gave me a head of steam going into Grammy week. Jason and I flew out to L.A. in February, as friends again. When the plane landed, I was transported from Manhattan's fifty shades of winter gray to a place greener and gaudier than the Garden of Eden.

At the Beverly Hills Hotel, flowers bloomed fragrantly around manicured walkways; a sparkling swimming pool reflected the scorched desert sky; skinny palm trees shot up on the horizon like emerald fireworks. The hotel had bungalows in back—little cabins nestled in the shade of verdant elephant ears and lush hibiscus. These bungalows were reserved for the big fish. Tommy and Donnie each had one, and I made my way back to see the former before my interview with the latter.

As I strolled through the secret garden, contemplating the trouble I could get in if anyone at Atlantic found out, who should come strolling in the opposite direction but Ahmet, arm in arm with a hooker. I recognized her; she was one of his favorites. We exchanged greetings and kept walking. *I won't tell your secret*, I thought. *You don't need to know mine.* He didn't seem to care anyway. He wasn't thinking with his brain just then.

Tommy answered his door wearing a tracksuit—not a flattering look for a man of his proportions.

"I just ran into Ahmet," I said.

"I bet he was with a hooker."

"How did you know?" I asked. He just laughed. Then, getting down to business, he said, "We want a woman in the A&R Department at Columbia. Go talk to Donnie and come back here when you're done."

I went to see Donnie. He was tall and handsome, filling the door of his bungalow as he ushered me in. He attempted idle chitchat, but I quickly realized he didn't want an interview so much as an audience. He talked and talked and talked—about his days at Arista with the iconic Clive Davis, who taught him that everything comes down to the song; about how many hits he had signed; about Columbia's future. Then he played a song called "Vision of Love," by an artist named Mariah Carey.

"I have big plans for her," Donnie said.

He wasn't kidding. The song would win a Grammy Award for Best Female Pop Vocal Performance the following year, and Mariah Carey would become, well, *Mariah Carey.*

"I'm working on a similar artist," I said. "It's Jason's project. Fiona."

"She'll never make it," Donnie said.

I was a little surprised by his honesty, but I loved it. He was right, too. She didn't make it. The interview ended, we shook hands and said good-bye, and I left with two feelings: Donnie Ienner was one of the most impressive men I had ever met, and I could never work with him. I went back to Mottola's bungalow and reported in, but I let the matter drop after that. I didn't want to leave Atlantic, and I certainly didn't want to work for Donnie at Columbia.

———————

After Grammy week, Jason and I returned to find Manhattan still submerged in the dead of winter. February drifted into March. From our ninth-floor office windows, all we could see was an endless landscape of skeleton trees dotting the slush-filled streets. The hangover after sunny Los Angeles was too much to bear. We needed a little hair of the dog.

Every March the dance-music industry held an event called the Winter Music Conference in Miami. Jason had a dance artist named Alta Dustin, and that gave us enough cover for the trip. We decided to make like snowbirds and fly south, the line between friend and boss blurring yet again.

In Miami, we mingled with DJs, artists, and executives from other labels' dance departments. During this mingling, I met a man who changed my life almost as drastically as Ahmet had. Joey Carvello, director of promotion at WTG Records, was handsome and over six feet tall. He had deep brown eyes, long brown curly hair, a lithe frame, and an aura of manic energy. I fell immediately in lust. We exchanged information and began calling each other incessantly. We made plans to go on a date when I came to L.A. again in April.

Our first date wasn't exactly a date; it was more like a series of invisible red flags. As soon as I arrived at my hotel, I received a message from Joey's office. He had thrown out his back and was in the hospital having an operation. I went to the hospital and met him in his room. He was sweet and vulnerable, and I was smitten. He didn't tell me that he had a girlfriend, or that he was currently living with another woman, or that he was still married to his first wife. He didn't tell me he drank heavily and dabbled in drugs. I thought the worst thing about him was that he smoked cigarettes. He did tell me that he could get airplay for Alta Dustin, the dance act Jason and I were struggling to promote. From his hospital bed, he picked up a phone, called a radio DJ, and proved his point. In the A&R world, that counted as foreplay. It definitely turned me on.

In the hospital, we decided we were a couple. Over the next few months, I flew around the country to join him wherever he was working. I caught glimpses of his dark side on these trips, but I didn't care. I wanted to be with him. I was falling in love, and for the first time, it seemed pure. We had to wait for sex due to his back operation; this made our relationship feel like the opposite of every one I'd known in the music business, where the only real goals were fucking and power. His charm worked on me. Even after I learned about his wife I still pursued him.

So much for purity.

17

GAME OF THRONES

By 1989, IT WAS CLEAR that Ahmet couldn't run Atlantic much longer. He still held the titles of chairman and CEO, but his role had diminished as his interest in the label waned. Doug now shouldered the day-to-day workload, and Sheldon controlled the purse strings. Everyone assumed Ahmet would choose one of them as his successor.

From my point of view, Sheldon had no chance. He was repellent. He treated people like shit. And those were his good qualities. Doug had every advantage. His longtime assistant, Joan Brooks, was Noreen Woods's sister, and Noreen was like Ahmet's right hand. Joan and Noreen kept Doug apprised of Ahmet's thoughts and actions, and they also encouraged Ahmet to pick Doug as his successor.

Doug was also more cunning than Sheldon; he knew how to manipulate people. He could keep the entire business in his head, doling out numbers and figures from memory. And Doug was ruthless. A favorite sport of his was to pit two executives against each other, even if they were friends, and put his efforts behind the winner. He did it with Vince Faraci and Sylvia Rhone to see who would run Atlantic's East West Records (winner: Sylvia Rhone). He did it with Beau Hill and Jimmy Iovine, copresidents of Interscope (winner: Jimmy Iovine). He did it with Jason Flom and Craig Kallman at Atlantic (winner and still cochairman at Atlantic: Craig Kallman).

Doug did have a few serious problems, though: as much as he loved fucking with his employees, Ahmet loved fucking with him. In 1988, Ahmet hired Jerry Greenberg to run Atlantic's sister company, Atco Records. Jerry had been president of Atlantic in the 1970s, and everyone still remembered him as a great boss. He treated his employees with respect and honesty, and they wanted to succeed for him. He was cute, with a full head of gray hair, and had an infectious personality. To put it bluntly, we all liked Jerry better than we liked Doug.

Doug wouldn't have worried about a personality contest; what threatened him was that Jerry turned Atco into a powerhouse. While Doug was on the hook for Atlantic's failures, Jerry signed hit after hit, including British pop-rock band the Escape Club and female rap trio J. J. Fad. The Escape Club had a number one hit with "Wild, Wild West," and J. J. Fad's album went platinum, giving WEA its first platinum rap album. This was an extra thorn in Doug's side—he had long been trying to move Atlantic away from rock music and into rap/dance music. He had groomed Sylvia Rhone for just that purpose, with little to show for it.

Doug must have known he was in trouble when Jerry came back to New York. As the heir apparent, and the former president of Atco, Doug should have been offered the job, or at least Ahmet should have installed a figurehead. Instead Ahmet brought in a serious contender. This left Doug with only one option: get rid of Jerry Greenberg.

Here's where it gets fishy. In 1989 Tommy Mottola teamed up with CBS head honcho Walter Yetnikoff to create a new label in California under the Sony umbrella, and he asked Jerry to be its president. He flattered Jerry, calling the label WTG, for Walter, Tommy, and Gerald. Jerry ditched Atco and moved back to California. Ahmet saw it as the ultimate betrayal, and the threat to Doug was neutralized.

I don't know for sure that Doug orchestrated this move, but I believe he had something to do with it. No other explanation fits the facts. There was no reason for Tommy to create WTG except to help Doug. He already had Sony and Epic. Also, the timing was suspiciously convenient—at the exact moment Doug needed a favor, his friend Tommy showed up with just the thing. Doug knew that Jerry hated the East Coast (that's why Jerry left Atlantic in 1980, opening the job for Doug in the first place). Doug also knew Jerry had come back to New York only as a favor to Ahmet, and that he longed to get back to his home in California. Doug probably guessed that Jerry would leave Atco if the right opportunity presented itself. So Tommy made Jerry an offer he couldn't refuse. Tommy would have understood the value of having Doug Morris owe him a favor. Favors go a long way at the top—for instance, when Tommy got fired from Sony in 2003 for failing to produce hits, Doug gave him $50 million to start his own label at Universal Music Group, where Doug was then chairman and CEO.

Again, I can't say for sure that this is what happened, but from my experience in the business, it makes sense. I witnessed the ways these men would close ranks to protect each other. I saw how they rigged the system so they couldn't fail, even when they failed. As much as they'd fuck each other over, they'd also prop each other up.

What Doug did next gives further credence to my version of the story. It also shows how nasty he could be. Jerry Greenberg had a nephew named Kenny Komisar, director of Atlantic's Dance Department. Kenny was helping keep Atlantic afloat with dance hits, while Doug floundered in the rock market. Doug fired him. Then, to fill the position, Doug set his sights on Jerry's best promotion man at WTG. These were Mafia-like maneuvers. I believe Doug was essentially sending a message to the other capos of the music business: *If you fuck with me, I'll take you out of the picture, fire your family, and steal your best employee.*

Whatever truly happened, Doug had another major problem to deal with: Steve Ross, the head of Time Warner, didn't like him. After Jerry left Atco, Ross didn't even approach Doug about what to do at the label. Instead he sought out Derek Shulman, the senior vice president of A&R at Polygram Records. Derek was on a hot streak with Tears for Fears, Cinderella, Dexys Midnight Runners, Men Without Hats, and more. Steve Ross even enlisted Ahmet's help to woo Derek, and Ahmet came through with a trip to his villa in Turkey. Derek accepted the position at Atco, and another gladiator entered Doug's ring.

Their first battle came over AC/DC. Despite the band's status as rock 'n' roll royalty their sales were slipping. Their deal had come up on Atlantic, and Doug wanted to drop them. Derek made a deal for AC/DC on Atco, and their next record, *Blow Up Your Video*, went platinum.

Point, Derek.

Derek had also inherited the deal Jerry Heller made with R&B singer (and Dr. Dre's girlfriend) Michel'le. Dr. Dre produced her album, and like everything he touched at that time, it went gold. Atco also had hits from Pantera, the Rembrandts, Dream Theater, and Bad Company. Ahmet noticed. He became close with Derek and seemed to lose faith in Doug.

Doug had lost the battle but not the war. Like a great general, he was massing his troops, watching the field, and waiting until he had the advantage. The field would become much more complicated with the merger between Time and Warner in 1989, and the appearance of Bob Morgado as chairman of Warner Music Group (Doug would set his sights on Morgado's job in the mid-1990s, but it would prove to be his Waterloo). For now, Doug had already made his first tactical maneuver by pursuing WTG's best promotion executive. This would turn out to be a brilliant move for Doug. It was also an unexpected calamity for me. The executive in question was none other than my new boyfriend, Joey Carvello.

18

THE TENDER TRAP

In June, I was on my way to meet Joey for the weekend when Jason called and said, "Doug wants to interview Joey for the Dance Department job. Don't fuck this up. Use your charm to close the deal." I understood that to mean sex. I was banging Joey anyway; what the hell else could I do? I felt so sick of these men. After everything I had done to claw my way to a position of legitimacy, they acted like the only thing I could do was bang someone for favors. This treatment started to break me down.

More trouble soon came my way. I went to Boca Raton, Florida, to meet Joey at a conference, and while there, I ran into my old friend Michael Lippman. Michael managed pop superstar George Michael, but I knew him from way back, outside the business. One night in Florida, Michael invited me to dinner with a few of his industry friends. Among those friends was Dennis Lavinthal, cofounder of *Hits* magazine, a trade publication that acted more like an independent promotion company. Dennis wrote a gossip column under the pen name I. B. Bad, and everyone in the business read it.

During dinner, Michael told Dennis that I had signed Skid Row.

"I *helped* sign them," I said, correcting him. "Jason Flom was the A&R rep who signed them, and without him, I wouldn't have been promoted." We finished dinner, and I forgot about the whole thing.

A few months later, I had a mild surgical procedure and was home recuperating when Jason called me. "Have you read *Hits*?" he asked. I could tell he was angry.

"No, I'm home recovering," I said. I heard some paper rustling in the background, and Jason began to read: "All accolades on Dorothy Sicignano for signing Skid Row."

"Did you put that in there?" Jason demanded.

I almost laughed. I couldn't believe he was serious.

"Doug is furious," Jason continued. "Why isn't my name in there?"

I told Jason what had happened at the dinner in Miami, and then I called Doug and repeated the story to him. I explained that I never asked *Hits* to write about me, and that I would never cut Jason out of a deal that everyone knew was partly his. I urged them to call Michael Lippman, certain he would vouch for me.

Doug ordered me to stay away from the media in the future, and I apologized. After hanging up, I threw out the bouquet of get-well flowers that Doug, Jason, and Tunc had sent me, and returned to bed.

I couldn't stand these men much longer. Jason's two-faced behavior was hard enough to accept, but Doug was like Dr. Jekyll and Mr. Hyde. When he found out that I couldn't afford my medical procedure (insurance wouldn't cover it, and it cost $1,000), he cut me a bonus check. He even calculated for taxes so that I'd receive exactly what I needed. It was one of the sweetest things anyone had ever done for me. But after the *Hits* misunderstanding, Doug began treating me like a traitor. He planted a seed in Jason's mind—*Dorothy is working against you; don't trust her*—and the seed found fertile soil.

———

In August, Doug went to L.A. and offered Joey the Dance Department job at double his WTG salary. He wanted Joey to move to Manhattan immediately; Doug would pay all moving expenses and apartment rental fees. Joey arrived in New York with a six-figure salary, a team of four people under him, and a room at the Omni Berkshire Hotel until he found an apartment.

It all happened so fast I didn't have time to consider what it would mean for me. I had no lack of warning signs, though. Joey's first wife wrote me a letter in which she blamed me for everyone Joey ever banged and said I was a horrible person. I was shocked, but I ignored it. In hindsight, I should have listened to her warning. It taught me an important lesson: the first wife has seen the dirty laundry; learn from her.

The next warning sign came when Joey told me he was having trouble with his credit cards. I volunteered to give him an Amex card on my credit line. His first month's bill topped $4,000, all spent on bullshit living expenses. At first, he paid these bills on time. As months went by, though, he began paying them later and later. He always had a convincing excuse—his first wife sued him for divorce and wanted a settlement, or he had outstanding taxes—but the truth was, he put his financial needs before mine, and I let it happen. As a result, while he straightened out his credit, mine became ruined.

I had no financial training and little idea of what credit meant. This problem was far bigger, and older, than me. For most of recorded history, women couldn't possess their own wealth. Even if a woman somehow broke through these restrictions, her money became her husband's property after marriage. By the 1980s, women had begun digging themselves out of this hole and demanding a place in the economy, but you can't just undo centuries of repression. It takes time, and training, and access. I didn't have time, no one offered me training, and my access was limited to men who thought of me as an object, if they thought of me at all.

The problem went beyond gender. I came from the lowest rung of the middle class. My family didn't have credit cards or stock options. We lived paycheck to paycheck. As an A&R executive, my salary included stock in the company, but I had no idea what stock was. Unlike Jason or Ahmet, I didn't have a father who handed me money and taught me how it worked. I was playing a dangerous game without knowing the rules.

A few months after Joey moved to New York, his credit card bill skyrocketed to $50,000. He now made more than double my salary, but this time he didn't offer to pay at all. The red flags weren't so invisible anymore.

One night at the Omni Berkshire, I was folding a pair of Joey's pants, waiting for him to come home, when out of the pocket fell a small vial filled with what looked like drugs. To make sure, I took the vial to Jason's apartment, and he confirmed it. I confronted Joey the next day. He said it wasn't his, and I believed him. It was the answer I wanted to hear.

Joey had a knack for smoothing things over. Soon after the incident, he called me into his office to give me a Jack Russell terrier puppy named Bijou. He knew I loved dogs, and he could pick them as well as he could pick a hit record—the breed would soon explode in popularity. I forgot about the drugs.

In September, Joey and I decided to move to Brooklyn so he could avoid the temptation of staying out late, partying, and doing drugs. We moved into a brownstone in Park Slope, but it didn't help. Addiction isn't a choice. It doesn't respect boundaries. Joey was going to do whatever he wanted to do even if we moved to the moon.

When he was high he was zero fun. He slept all the time. I felt like a hostage in my own home. We began to argue. He spent his days on cloud nine while I was the sober one dealing with a mountain of bills—his bills. He went out nearly every night, and sometimes he didn't come home. When I asked about it, he resented me. I assumed he had something to hide, but he wouldn't tell me. Desperation set in. I should have left. Instead, I did the opposite.

In late November, Doug called me into the conference room. I went downstairs and found him seated at the big conference table, flanked by Tunc, Jason, and Joey. "Joey wants to ask you something," Doug said. Joey stood up and said, "Will you marry me?"

I said yes and ran over to hug and kiss Doug (he was holding the ring; I had my eye on the prize). I grabbed the ring and kissed Joey. Tunc poured all of us glasses of champagne and we toasted to the future.

I guess I thought Joey would change if we settled down, so I rushed to get married. We set the date for December 3, 1989. As the news spread, I got a call from one of Joey's friends, Boston DJ John Luongo. "Don't marry Joey," he said. "The two of you are nitroglycerin in a blender."

"I can handle it," I replied.

Of course, Joey had to get divorced first, but that barely registered for me. This whole time I saw myself as morally superior to Ahmet and Doug for the way they conducted their personal lives, and yet it never even occurred to me what a hypocrite I was, taking what I wanted at the expense of another woman's feelings.

I married Joey on Sunday, December 3, 1989, at the Saint Moritz hotel overlooking Central Park. It was a small wedding. We both went to work the next day; I would never dream of missing a day at Atlantic just because I got married. We had no honeymoon period, either. Within weeks, our relationship collapsed. It didn't take long for my career at Atlantic to get pulled down into the wreckage. Instant karma.

———————

Around this time, Kalodner decided to reappear. He invited me to lunch and apologized for the way he had treated me. It came as a shock; no one in this business apologized, least of all Kalodner. He said I was the nicest of the nice people he had ever known, and he regretted the way he had acted. I accepted his apology. It felt nice to have him back.

On New Year's Eve 1989, Skid Row opened for Aerosmith at the Boston Garden. I took Joey, since he was from Boston. Jason went too. When we arrived, we met up with Tim Collins, Kalodner, and his girl-friend Samantha. There we were, the dysfunctional little family, ushering in 1990 together. When we got to the Garden, Joey was already wired to the max. At some point during the show, he disappeared. I was furious. I had plenty of company, but my husband ditched me on New Year's Eve.

After the show, Joey was nowhere in sight. I returned to an empty hotel room. Around 3:00 AM, the door creaked open and Joey stumbled through it. I flew at him, and we battled nose to nose.

"Are you high?" I demanded.

"No," he lied.

"Who the fuck were you with?"

"None of your fucking business!"

"I'm leaving!"

As I turned to walk out of the room he picked up an ashtray and threw it at me as hard as he could. It slammed into my back. I was stunned. This was different from when Ahmet fractured my forearm. This was the man I was supposed to spend the rest of my life with. What pissed me off most was that it was a cheap shot from behind. I bolted into the hallway, called Tim Collins, and asked if I could come to his room. He kindly let me in, and I told him what happened. We agreed I should stay away from Joey for the night.

The next morning, Tim invited us to a New Year's Day brunch in a private room. I returned to my room to shower and change. Joey was asleep. I went to the brunch alone, ashamed that this had happened to me. I hardly tasted the food as my mind raced with questions: *How can I stay with a man who would do something like that? How can I end the marriage after three weeks? How would it look to everyone, especially Doug, and Ahmet, and my peers at Atlantic? What would my parents think? What would Sister Rose Ellen say?* Divorce was forbidden in the Catholic Church, and I still felt that tremendous guilt. I also felt the shame of failure. Ahmet always said I couldn't keep a man. Maybe he was right.

In the end, my ego took over. I couldn't admit I had made the wrong choice. I couldn't admit my marriage was a sham, finished as soon as it began. I went back to my hotel room after brunch and found Joey awake. I wanted to talk about what had happened, but I didn't say anything. Years later, after we divorced, I brought it up. He said he couldn't remember anything from that night. I'd heard that one before.

19

SUCKA PUNCH

I LIMPED INTO THE NEW year. The American Express card bill hit $70,000, and I had no way to pay it off. I tried to get a loan and failed. Desperate, I turned to Joey. Despite his six-figure salary, he didn't offer to fix his mess. He imparted two words of advice: file bankruptcy. I implicitly accepted his financial burden. Maybe it stemmed from a character flaw in me, or maybe it was the lingering message from my childhood that men were more important than me, but I thought I had to do it.

Bankruptcy erased the debt, but it also wiped out my credit for ten years. I didn't expect that. I stared ahead at a decade of penance for my husband's sins, a decade in which I couldn't get a loan, couldn't buy a house or a car, couldn't even get a credit card, making it almost impossible to do my job, which involved crisscrossing the country and even the world. It was a bitter fucking pill.

As the reality of bankruptcy set in, a quiet rage built up inside me. I didn't yet have the self-knowledge to understand this rage, so it came out in silent little ways. For instance, I refused to file my taxes with Joey's. We fought constantly. Resentment slowly replaced intimacy. Instead of husband and wife we became adversaries. Our marriage was bankrupt.

It didn't help that every record Joey touched seemed to turn gold. He became the star at Atlantic. People started kissing his ass, and I got attention only when someone needed to find him. When my office phone rang, more often than not, the voice on the other end would say, "Where's Joey?" I felt like his secretary, and I hated it.

Doug loved having Joey around. He had long wanted Atlantic to move away from rock music and toward dance, pop, and rhythm music. That's where the trend was heading, and he saw it. Unfortunately the new head of promotion, Andrea Ganis, didn't see it. She set the priorities for promotion at Atlantic, which meant she controlled which songs the label put its weight behind. As her boss, Doug could have just ordered her to change the priorities, but Doug never took the direct approach. Instead he used Joey as a disruptor. He told Joey to sign dance records, undermining Doug's own Promotion Department but pushing Atlantic in the direction he wanted it to go. When Ganis got angry, she'd get angry with Joey, not Doug.

If that were Doug's only move, it would have been effective but not impressive. What truly made Doug a brilliant manipulator was his incredible vision. He was playing a complex game of chess, and like any chess master, he could see the whole game at once. Doug had already demonstrated that he wanted to make Sylvia Rhone a success at any cost, so he put Joey under her. In this way, Doug not only moved the label where he wanted it to go while avoiding Ganis's wrath, he also accomplished his goal with Sylvia. In other words, with just one move of his pawn (Joey), Doug protected his queen (Sylvia) and set up the board (Atlantic) on his terms.

Here's an example of how it worked: Sylvia was trying to break the female R&B group En Vogue. During a promotion meeting, Sylvia touted the group to Doug as her signature project. She felt sure it was a hit, but Ganis disagreed. In order to force Ganis's hand, Sylvia had to get the record to cross over from R&B radio to pop radio.

Here we must pause to explain the term "cross over" and all this fuss about dance music, R&B music, and pop music. From the advent of audio recording, popular music was divided into two categories: mainstream records and race records. With few exceptions, race records—that is, anything by a black artist—rarely received mainstream radio play. This severely limited the money that could be made in black music, which in turn limited the money a label put behind it. By the 1980s, the terms had changed. Instead of race records, we called them rhythm, or

R&B, or dance records. But the effect was the same: white music and black music remained separate entities (even though there would have been little white music of the past century without black music). MTV followed the same rules, rarely giving airplay to black artists, making a crossover hit even harder to come by.

That's where Joey came in. He had a savant-like ability to make a record cross over. He could pick the song and know which of his radio contacts to lean on to get it played. Following Doug's orders, he worked En Vogue's first single, "Hold On," for Sylvia. She delivered the R&B stations, and he got enough pop stations on board that Ganis had no choice but to put the Promotion Department behind it. In February 1990, "Hold On" went to the top of the dance chart and hit number two on the mainstream *Billboard* Hot 100. The song became the top R&B hit (and number eight pop hit) for the entire year.

Checkmate.

Unfortunately, what made Joey so great at his job also made him a pain in the ass. No one could manage him. The drugs didn't help. He was a ball of wiry, manic energy, impossible to contain. He began stepping on Sylvia's toes, signing dance hit after dance hit and getting them all to cross over, while she had only En Vogue to her name. The success went to his head, and Sylvia turned on him. Sylvia approached Mojo Nicosia, one of Joey's employees, and asked him to tell her when Joey did drugs in the office so she could catch him and fire him. This was clearly a hatchet job. If she really thought Joey had a drug problem, she had a professional and moral obligation to offer him a place in a rehab facility. If he refused, then she had the right to fire him. Ultimately, Mojo couldn't be disloyal to Joey, and he told him Sylvia's plot.

That wasn't the end of it, however, although again, the chess master worked behind the scenes, leaving me with nothing but traces and hunches. The next year, Joey signed a dance act called Bingoboys, and their single, "How to Dance," took off. MTV put the video in rotation, and it looked like the record would go gold, but after 450,000 units sold (just 50,000 shy of a gold record), Doug decided to make it a cut-out.

To understand what a dick move that was, recall the industry practice of cut-outs. When a label had a flop, they'd take the unsold records retailers had returned, punch a hole or add a notch to the album cover, and then resell the cut-outs at a discounted price. These usually wound up in a bargain bin, helping the label recoup some money from a failed project. In other words, you wouldn't cut-out a record just before it went gold unless you wanted to fuck with someone. I believe this was a warning shot from Doug. He liked Joey, but he wasn't going to let Joey threaten Sylvia. Again, Doug wanted to make Sylvia look good at all costs. Joey, naturally, didn't get the message.

While Joey's fortunes rose, mine sank. In late 1989 I had signed a band called Hericane Alice (we had to spell it funny to avoid legal trouble with the band Hurricane). Hericane Alice's album came out in early 1990, and it sank like a stone. Stiffs are a part of any A&R person's job, but to fail while my husband succeeded only increased my resentment for him.

Then the Hericane Alice debacle got worse. Jimmy Iovine comanaged the band with Glen Parrish, and the album was recorded at A&M studios, where Jimmy was the manager. In March, after the record flopped, Doug called me to his office and handed me a bill from Jimmy for independent publicity for Hericane Alice. Doug sat with his feet on his desk, brushing the sides of his hair as he often did. "Call Jimmy up and tell him that Atlantic does not pay for independent publicity," he said. "And don't mention my name." I dreaded this call, but it was a direct order from my boss. On the phone, Jimmy and I exchanged pleasantries and I informed him that Atlantic would not pay the bill and that he needed preapproval in the future. I spoke respectfully, even deferentially, because I knew how close he was to Doug. He hung up on me.

A few minutes later Doug called me back to his office. He was laughing. "You fucked with Jimmy, and now he wants me to fire you," Doug said. My heart sank. After that, Jimmy Iovine blackballed me. He never took my calls again, and he even badmouthed me to Paul Marshall, an attorney in the music business. I took it personally.

Years later, I went out for drinks with publicist Melanie A. Bonvicino and Suge Knight, cofounder of Death Row Records. At the time, Suge was one of the scariest men in the business. He's still pretty scary—as of this writing he's awaiting a murder trial. He told me there were only two people he feared: Jimmy Iovine and Doug Morris.

At work, I became increasingly isolated. Doug, it seemed, only spoke to me to fuck with me. Ahmet remained a background presence. I couldn't really call Jason my friend anymore. At home, I became increasingly desperate. Joey and I were locked in constant battle. We fought more than we talked. I rarely smiled anymore. I became paranoid. Sometimes I struggled to breathe.

In September, Joey and I decided to move back to the city. He wanted an easier commute to work, but I could only see the expense. It's not that I loved Brooklyn and wanted to live there forever—at the time, Park Slope was not the celebrity-filled yuppie neighborhood it is today, and I had my car stolen twice—but Manhattan cost real money, and we were struggling. Regardless, we moved.

Joey hit Manhattan hard. He often didn't come home at night, and I often felt relieved when I didn't see him. I also felt guilty about feeling this. I was failing. I didn't mind failing at a job. I could always get a new one. But failing at a relationship meant I had failed as a person. Nearly every woman I knew—from my mother to my aunts to the few women who had succeeded in the business—stayed with assholes. They made it work for decades. Why couldn't I make it work for even one year? Why couldn't I accept that men got to do whatever they wanted, and women had to stand by them? One of Ahmet's favorite lessons came back into my mind: "Men biologically can't be faithful." Maybe Ahmet was right. I just had to deal with it. It came as no surprise to me that Joey was seeing other women. After all, when we started dating, he was still married. How you get them is how you lose them—I learned that one the hard way. But I couldn't deal with it.

One night when Joey didn't come home, I waited up for him, preparing for the confrontation I could no longer hold back. It was nearly 7:00 AM when he straggled through the door, drunk and high. We assumed battle positions. I yelled at him, and he bent down to my height and shoved his face in mine. "If you don't shut your big mouth, I'll shut it for you," Joey screamed. I hated being threatened. It offended me more than anything.

LEFT: With Jason Flom at a Grammy party, 1988. RIGHT: Ahmet Ertegun and Jason Flom at the Peabody Hotel, 1988. *Dorothy Carvello*

Backstage with Aerosmith manager Tim Collins, Hawaii, 1988. *Courtesy of Tim Collins*

With Vito Bratta of White Lion and Steven Tyler of Aerosmith on tour in Honolulu, Hawaii, 1988. *Dorothy Carvello*

Doug Morris and Ahmet Ertegun, 1987. *Courtesy of Janice Roeg*

Janice Roeg with Noreen Woods, Ahmet's longtime assistant, 1987. *Courtesy of Janice Roeg*

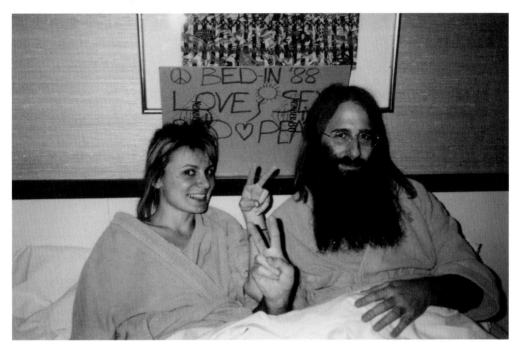

With John Kalodner at the "Bed In"—an impromptu re-creation of the famous photo of John Lennon and Yoko Ono at the UN Plaza Hotel. Photo taken by Jason Flom. *Dorothy Carvello*

Joey DeMaio of Manowar and John Kalodner, Los Angeles, 1997. *Courtesy of Joey DeMaio for All About E, LLC*

On the balcony of the Ritz-Carlton,
Palm Springs, 1988. *Dorothy Carvello*

Ahmet Ertegun and his girlfriend, Janice Roeg, 1987.
Courtesy of Janice Roeg

Joey Carvello with his artists Pajama Party, Jellybean, and Alta Dustin, at Winter Music Conference, 1990. *Courtesy of Joseph Carvello*

With Joey Carvello, Manhattan, 1989. *Dorothy Carvello*

Larry Yasgar, former VP of dance music and single sales at Atlantic, seen here in his office at Vendetta/A&M Records, 1990. *Courtesy of Joseph Carvello*

With Jon Bon Jovi and Sebastian Bach on tour in Dallas, Texas, January 1989. *Dorothy Carvello*

Michael Hutchence at Wembley Stadium, 1991. *Courtesy of Petrol Records*

Charlie Minor and his daughter, Austin. *Dorothy Carvello*

Randy Goodman, senior vice president of marketing at RCA, a.k.a. Senior VP McDreamy. *Courtesy of Randy Goodman*

Left to right: Bob Morgado, Linda Moran, and Michael Fuchs at Moran's fiftieth birthday party at Chesarina in New York City, 1995. *Courtesy of Linda Moran*

With Jerry Blair at my birthday party
at John's Pizza in New York City, 2000.
Dorothy Carvello

With Richie Sambora at a Skid Row
concert, New Jersey, 1997. *Dorothy
Carvello*

Don Ienner in 2008 in his house in Green-
wich, Connecticut. *Courtesy of Don Ienner*

I wanted to hurt him. I jumped on the couch to take away his height advantage, faked him with my right hand, and hit him in the eye with my left fist. He reeled back, stunned not so much from the punch as from the fact that I had hit him. I didn't feel sorry, and I didn't apologize. On some level, I felt I had evened the score for the ashtray incident. My hand throbbed from the punch. The pain cleared my mind, and I realized that if he hit me back, I could get seriously hurt—he was six foot four and had a black belt in karate. I fled the scene.

A few hours later I came home and changed for work. Joey was gone. At the office, I found him wearing dark glasses and telling everyone I gave him a black eye. Doug called me into his office and shouted at me: "Stop hitting my executives! What's wrong with you?" Doug never once asked if Joey hit me, if he threatened me, or if I felt afraid to go home that night. He didn't say a word about seeking professional help. Doug had helped so many of his employees with major life issues, including Jason, but he offered me nothing. Instead, he sent me back into the abusive environment from which I came, and he made me feel tremendous guilt for what had happened. It was a classic case of blaming the victim—no matter what my husband did, the only problem was that I retaliated. The message, at least to me, came across loud and clear: I was unworthy of Doug's help.

If that seems melodramatic, consider this: just a few months before I punched Joey, Vince Faraci, senior vice president of promotion, cold-cocked his secretary in the office. Doug saw the whole thing happen from the hallway. He responded by promoting Faraci to executive vice president of Atlantic. It was a passive-aggressive way to get rid of him—just move him to another part of the building—but I didn't get the passive-aggressive treatment, and I sure as hell didn't get a promotion. In fact, Doug couldn't stop laughing while he reprimanded me. As Doug led me out of his office, he said, "Get back to work," and he ducked like I was going to hit him. Even I had to laugh, if only to cover the humiliation.

After I punched Joey in the face, all the men in the office acted like they were afraid of me. They called me tough, intimidating, and rough. It hurt my feelings. I saw myself as misunderstood. I felt like a nice person on the inside, but they could only see the tense, anxious, sad, stressed, besieged person on the outside. I didn't yet have the wisdom to understand how my actions influenced the way others saw me. The reactions I got—from Doug, from Joey, and from the other men in the office—led me to believe that the only way I could get a man to listen to me was to use my fists. I was crying for help, but I got laughed at instead.

20

KNOCKOUT

In late September Jason called an A&R meeting. The department had just moved to new offices on the third floor of the Sperry Rand Building on Sixth Avenue, which connected to the third floor of Atlantic's offices at 75 Rockefeller Plaza. When I entered Jason's new office, he was chomping on a cigar and cracking jokes with the other executives. He looked at me, patted his thighs, and said, "Honey, come sit on my lap." Then, with the biggest grin, he said it again: "Honey, come sit on my lap." My face burned with embarrassment. Since my promotion to A&R, I had heard whispers that I had fucked Jason to get my job. On top of everything else I had gone through, to have him add fuel to that rumor was too much to bear. It was the ultimate invalidation, both of our friendship and of my worth as an executive. Everyone laughed except Frankie LaRocca, who said, "Leave her alone." I could barely move from the shock. Then something in me snapped.

"What the fuck is wrong with you?" I spat. "I'm not sitting on your fucking lap."

I ran to the bathroom and cried bitter, furious tears. The realizations came thick and fast: I would always be a secretary, a cunt, and a nothing with these men. I had enabled them to treat me poorly and without respect. I didn't even know what respect was or how to get it—I had so rarely witnessed it in my life. If I didn't do something to stop it now, it would never end.

I composed myself and went to the second floor to see Linda Moran, a senior vice president at Atlantic. She'd worked at Atlantic for years and knew where the bodies were buried. I told her what had happened and she advised me to tell Doug. I decided to say it with a memo—it was easier than crying in front of him—and Linda volunteered to type so my assistant wouldn't see it. She knew that Atlantic treated women like shit, and I think she needed to get it off her chest as much as I did. Linda typed fast:

> Dear Doug,
> Today during an A&R meeting called by the department VP, Jason Flom, I was singled out as the only female and was asked to sit on his lap in front of the entire staff. I am a married woman, and my husband works for you. After my contributions to the company, and my loyalty to you and Ahmet, why do I have to go through this bullshit? Not one man in this place would ask your friend and protégé, Sylvia Rhone, to sit on their lap. They would be too scared. I'm tired of this juvenile behavior by all the men at Atlantic Records. It's a free for all in this place. Please let me know what you intend to do about it. Thank you.

The following morning I received a message that Ahmet and Doug wanted to see me at the end of the day to discuss the memo. When 4:00 PM rolled around I found Ahmet pacing nervously around his office. Doug wasn't there. Ahmet left for a few minutes and came back muttering, "I can't believe Doug expects me to do his dirty work." I was confused. Then Ahmet said, "How can you write a memo like that and expect to work here? After all, what's his name [Jason] is all we got. Doug wants you to resign immediately."

"I'm not resigning," I said. "Why should I have to sit on his lap?"

"Resign or Doug will fire you," Ahmet said.

"But I didn't do anything wrong," I said.

"Doug says you questioned his authority. I can't believe you are so dumb to do this to Doug. This isn't how it was supposed to end with us. This is not what I want. You leave me no choice."

"But, Ahmet, you can save me," I pleaded.

"No way. Doug says you're gone. Go see the furniture lady"—Ahmet's nickname for the VP of human resources—"and work out an exit package."

After leaving Ahmet's office, I went upstairs, feeling rejected and overwhelmed with guilt and regret. I was also devastated. I had just lost my job and a huge part of my identity. I asked the woman in personnel for three months' severance pay and filed for unemployment. Doug agreed to the terms, and I went down to clean out my office. I packed gold records, files, and phone numbers, all while saying strained good-byes to the guys in A&R. Wendy Berry came in and asked how she could get my job. I had no problem with Wendy, but it was an insensitive question, so I gave her an insensitive answer: "Show Jason your tits. It's all he ever talks about."

Looking back on it, I never felt angry with Ahmet. He didn't stand up for me, but I didn't blame him. He only stood up for himself; I knew that already. Doug, on the other hand, showed his true colors. He didn't even have the guts to be in the room when I got fired. I didn't feel angry with him until years later, though. At the time, Doug gaslit me so bad ("gaslighting" means manipulating someone into questioning her own memories, feelings, and experiences) that he had me convinced I had done something awful by writing the memo. It was the same bullshit I had gone through when I punched Joey. Men could act without consequence, but women reacted at their peril.

I wish I had shown more courage. I should have hired a lawyer to speak to Doug or at least pressured Doug to give me a job at one of the other labels under the Atlantic umbrella. I should have realized immediately how wrong they were to fire me for refusing to sit on a man's lap and speaking up about it. I should have realized what cowards Doug and Jason were by the way they acted during this whole ordeal. In addition to skipping out on my firing, Doug hurried Jason onto a plane to L.A. so he wouldn't have to see me before I left. But I was blinded by my shame.

A few weeks later I went to see Jason, and I apologized for getting him into trouble with Doug. He accepted my apology—*imagine that*— but he never apologized to me, even though I had lost my job because of him. Doug and Ahmet never apologized either. I don't think any of them felt the slightest twinge of guilt. In their worldview, which I shared at the time, I had crossed a line. I was a woman who had publicly questioned a male superior. They had to terminate me.

Women today still deal with the same bullshit. Luckily we have better ways of combating it, but the juvenile mind-set of corporate America persists. It's like a little clubhouse. When I began working at Atlantic, they had only just taken down the NO GIRLS ALLOWED sign, but women were still expendable. "Last hired, first fired," as the saying goes. The slightest misstep—like refusing to sit on a man's lap and airing a grievance about it—got you kicked out.

Had the scene with Jason happened today instead of in 1990, the end of the story would most likely have been reversed. He'd have been fired and apologized to me for his conduct. But even so, would I have gotten any closer to my dream? Could I have worked my way up to a position of real power? It's hard to say for sure. Sylvia Rhone did it—she became president of Motown and executive vice president of Universal Records—but looking at the broader trends, it seems unlikely. In 2015, according to the *New York Times*, fewer large companies were run by women than by men named John. As of this writing, women make up more than half of the US population but less than 7 percent of Fortune 500 CEOs (and that's the highest number since *Fortune* started keeping a list in 1955). Let's just say the odds weren't in my favor then, and they wouldn't be in my favor now.

All of this is moot, of course. It did happen in 1990, and I had no choice but to leave my job without knowing how I would support myself and pay off my husband's debt. Worse, leaving Atlantic was a sort of death. I lost my identity. Without Ahmet Ertegun, who was I?

PART II

GIANT/RCA

21

A DJ SAVED MY LIFE

AFTER MY INGLORIOUS EXIT FROM Atlantic, I avoided everyone in the music business for as long as I could. I stayed home nursing a bruised heart while I watched Joey leave for my dream job every morning. It gave me a new reason to resent him.

As for Jason, I reeled between missing him terribly and wanting revenge on him. I wanted revenge on Doug, too, but I didn't want to put Joey's job in jeopardy. I figured the best revenge would be a glorious comeback. I would show them exactly what they were missing. I didn't know how, but I had faith in myself, and I knew the god of hits would shine upon me again.

A few weeks later, I visited Joey at Atlantic. It felt strange to come back so soon. I felt like a trespasser, hugging the walls and darting around corners so no one saw me. Joey was in his office on the phone with Ralph Tashjian, an independent promoter from San Francisco. When I entered, Joey put Ralph on speakerphone.

"Hi, Ralph," I said. "I'm so bored. Do you have any records for me? I need a job."

"Yes, I do," he said. "I just got an account, Big Beat Records, and I'm getting a good response to one of their songs from KMEL in the Bay."

"Send it overnight!" I shouted.

The tape arrived the next day by Federal Express. The song was "Hold You Tight" by Tara Kemp. I popped it in, and as soon as I heard the catchy soul groove, I knew it was a hit. It was different from any-thing I'd worked on—I'd built my career on the juvenile swagger of hair metal—but genre made little difference to me. A hit was a hit was a hit.

Big Beat was owned by Craig Kallman. He started as a DJ in New York nightclubs while in high school, and during college he programmed urban and rock specialty shows for WBRU in addition to working as a rep for CBS Records. I got his number from Ralph—"He's just a kid," Ralph warned—and I called him immediately. "You have a hit record," I said. "I need to see you."

When I first laid eyes on Craig, I was completely smitten. He had big blue eyes and curly blond hair. He was only a few years younger than me, but Ralph was right: he seemed like a kid. He wore jeans and sneakers, and was shy and quiet. I was surprised that after so much experience in music he knew next to nothing about how the major labels worked. I told him I wanted to take Tara Kemp's record to Irving Azoff, and that if Irving didn't bite, we could try Doug Morris. "Who are they?" he said.

I smiled. At that moment, I knew I could be reinvented through Craig. He was like a virgin, unsullied by the music business. He had untapped executive potential: he was Ivy League educated, knew the numbers, and wasn't a pervert. I knew I could mold him into a formi-dable force, and I hoped I could keep him pure along the way.

I shared my hard-won wisdom with Craig, explaining how the majors worked and who the players were. I explained that Irving Azoff was the former manager of the Eagles and former president of MCA Records, and that he had just started a label called Giant Records. I'd learned enough about the business to know that a new label would be hungrier for artists than an established one. Also, as a new label, Giant could give all its attention to Tara Kemp's record. She wouldn't have to compete with any other acts. That was a huge selling point. Craig listened and learned.

No other man in the music business—not Ahmet, Doug, Jason, or Joey—mattered to me now. It was all Craig. We became inseparable. In a way, he replaced the void Jason had left in my life, but he replaced it with something better. I saw a future with Craig, and it made me feel better about myself than I had ever felt in the music business. We made a perfect team: I could pass all my street smarts and knowledge about the music business to him, and he could become one of the few decent men to hold a position of power.

The next day, I contacted Irving Azoff and told him about the Tara Kemp record. Irving asked me to come meet him in California. As word got out, Doug and Tommy Mottola both contacted Craig for meetings, but I felt Giant was the best place for us to go, and Craig trusted me.

Before leaving to meet Irving, I went back to Atlantic to pick up my last paycheck and ran into Ahmet. "What are you planning to do?" he asked. Apparently he felt concerned about me. Maybe he felt guilty—at least, if there's any justice in the world, he did.

"I'm going to L.A. to see Irving Azoff," I said.

"Is Azoff flying you out?"

"No," I admitted, and Ahmet looked at me with an expression of pity.

"Azoff isn't going to hire you," he said. "He's a scumbag."

"I know he's a scumbag, Ahmet, but I still need a job."

"You shouldn't fly out on your own money."

I didn't bother telling Ahmet what should have been obvious: because of him, I had no choice.

22

THE POISON DWARF

THEY CALLED IRVING AZOFF THE "Poison Dwarf." I had yet to experience the poison part, but at five foot three in shoes, he was one of the shortest men I'd ever seen. Irving was rumored to be the inspiration for Randy Newman's song "Short People": "*They got little hands / Little eyes / They walk around telling great big lies.*" I first met Irving in 1988 on a trip to Hawaii with John Kalodner, and I saw him occasionally at Atlantic whenever Doug wanted a raise. Irving had a reputation as the most evil man in the music business—David Geffen called him "devilish," and he wasn't being cute—but I'd dealt with devils before. Besides, at least Irving had a sense of humor. He named his company Giant Records, for Christ's sake.

We met in his Beverly Hills office on North Maple Drive. It was a corner office on a low floor, not too large, not too fancy. I went in feeling confident, armed with the strongest currency in the music business: a hit record. Irving wore California casual—a white button-down shirt and jeans—and the effect was disarming. I expected a man in corporate armor.

"I listened to your record," he said.

I nodded, so anxious I almost hated myself.

"You're right; it's a hit," he continued, "but I don't have any room for you."

I stared at him—his narrow face, his bushy eyebrows, his surprisingly bright blue eyes—and fought the familiar toss of my stomach. For me, there was no worse feeling than sitting across from a man who had complete power over me. I knew if I were a man with a hit record to sell, he'd hire me on the spot. I didn't let on that I knew this; after my experiences with Ahmet, Doug, and Jason, I was in no position to call it like I saw it anymore. Instead I tried some old-fashioned ass-kissing. "Everyone wants this record," I told Irving. "Tommy Mottola wants it. Doug Morris wants it. But I brought it to you."

"Dorothy, Dorothy," he said, holding up his hands as if to ward off my protest. "I don't have the budget for another A&R employee."

My heart sank.

"But . . ." he said, reconsidering, as my heart began reviving, "I need hits."

Giant had a full promotion staff with nothing to work on, and Irving was desperate to get the label running. He made a qualified offer: in return for Tara Kemp's record, he'd hire me as a consultant at $50,000 a year as soon as he could find an opening. I'd be treated as a full employee—expense account, money for travel, access to meetings and conferences. He'd also give me points on the record and a bonus if the record hit. He put me on the payroll right away, and I started work while my lawyer Peter Lopez negotiated my contract.

Irving and I called Craig together to make a bid on "Hold You Tight," which Craig accepted. Then Irving walked me around the Giant offices and introduced me to his staff. I saw my old friend Kenny Ostin, son of Warner Bros. CEO Mo Ostin, who had left Atlantic and now worked at Giant. His office was like an Arabian tent: he sat on pillows on the floor, chanting and meditating. It was a long way from when he had done a striptease down to his underwear on my desk at Atlantic. Irving's wife Shelli also worked in the building, but she didn't work for Giant. She represented soccer players (this was long before soccer was a blip on American pop culture's radar). I noticed on the thermostat a sign she had posted that read IF THE TEMPERATURE IS CHANGED TO GO ABOVE 68 DEGREES, YOU WILL BE FIRED—SHELLI AZOFF. I laughed to myself. That seemed like the Shelli I knew.

I had met her only once before, back in Hawaii with Kalodner, but she seemed smart and spoke her mind. She was petite and attractive, with long brown hair and a great figure. She and Irving made a refreshing alternative to Monique and Doug Morris—they were a fun-loving couple, youthful and rich. Sometimes he called her a cunt; sometimes she called him a prick. They were real.

Irving and I began our relationship on good terms. For his birthday, I sent a fruit basket to his Beverly Hills home. He sent me back a note that said: "Shelli got mad at me because I was throwing the fruit around the kitchen with the kids. Thank you for all the hits we are going to have together." I hung the note on my refrigerator.

In so many ways, Giant felt like a different world from Atlantic. I heard no discussions in the office about the stock market. I saw no ticker tape machines on anyone's desk. Irving didn't refer to people as peasants. The men didn't brag about their dicks or tell me to blow them. It was like breathing fresh air again after being trapped in a dungeon of greed and misogyny. I decided to come clean with Irving, knowing about his close relationship with Doug and wishing to start my new job on the right foot. I told him everything—about the meeting where Jason told me to sit on his lap, about the memo I wrote to Doug, and about the way they fired me. "That's sexual harassment," he said indignantly, implying he was above that sort of behavior. I couldn't help but notice that Irving had many female employees. Maybe he wasn't so poisonous after all.

I should have waited until I had a finalized contract before starting at Giant, but I jumped the gun on my comeback. I assumed everything would work out. Peter Lopez was a music-business attorney who also represented Glenn Frey of the Eagles, and I trusted him to negotiate my contract. He and his wife, Catherine Bach (better known as the original Daisy Duke), had come to my wedding. I never expected him to screw me.

I returned to New York feeling better than I had in months. The high continued in Giant's New York office, where I worked under Brian Koppelman. Brian's father cofounded SBK Entertainment World, which became the largest independent music publisher in the world. Like Jason, Brian was a Lucky Sperm. He was used to the finer things—he vacationed at Irving's Aspen home over the Christmas holiday—but to his credit, he acted nothing like the other A&R guys I had known. He wasn't envious of anyone's success. In fact, he tried to make my life easier. This courtesy was new to me.

Meanwhile, Craig and I grew closer. We had dinner together several nights a week, and Craig sought my advice on nearly everything, even on the girl he wanted to marry: Isabel Barbosa. Isabel was a stunning woman, with a figure straight out of *Vogue* magazine. Not only was she beautiful, she was a Brooklyn girl with a wicked sense of humor. She was smart, too, studying finance at Columbia University.

Craig invited her to one of our nightly dinners, and after she left, he said, "Should I ask her to marry me?"

"Craig," I answered, "I would close that deal as soon as possible."

Craig might have been the shy, nerdy type, but he knew how to woo a woman. He liked my lipstick, Lancôme Matte Red, and asked me where to buy it. I took him to the Lancôme counter at Barneys New York, and he bought an entire box for Isabel. Such attention to detail impressed me to no end. It must have impressed her too—they're still married.

Everything was working. I had the partner of my dreams in Craig, and I had bounced back from my worst nightmare at Atlantic to find myself stronger than before. Giant did a full-court press for Tara Kemp, spreading "Hold You Tight" from the Bay Area across the entire country, while I worked with Tara's producers to finish her album quickly so we could maximize the effect of radio play. I began traveling to Los Angeles for meetings and company conventions, and I already had another hot lead from Ralph Tashjian—a San Francisco rap duo called Sway and King Tech. I knew I could help Giant succeed. Maybe I could even realize my dream of becoming a vice president, or better.

My confidence soared after "Hold You Tight" hit the top spot on the dance chart and number three on the *Billboard* Hot 100 chart in January 1991. *Billboard* magazine described Tara as an artist with "the mass appeal of Paula Abdul" but with a better voice. I felt even more vindicated than I had with Skid Row.

It came as a surprise, then, when Irving Azoff abruptly stopped taking my calls. This should have been a red flag, but I was too busy working to recognize it. Then I got a call from a woman named Carol Fenelon, who worked in Giant's business affairs office.

"Stop calling Irving," she warned.

"What?"

"You're bothering him. We're not finishing your contract. You're fired."

"That's too bad," I said, getting heated, "because I gave him a hit record and I still haven't received my royalties."

"You're not getting anything."

I hung up, waited for my blood pressure to come down, and called Peter Lopez.

"You dragged your heels on getting this fucking contract done and now Azoff is dropping me!" I yelled.

"The contract will get done," he said. I wanted to believe him. Maybe he knew something I didn't.

"Call Azoff and find out what the hell is going on," I said and hung up.

In the meantime, I put a call in to Michael Lippman, my friend who had invited me to the dinner in Miami that led to the *Hits* debacle. Michael had survived a few run-ins with Azoff, and he always had his ear to the ground, so I asked him if he had heard anything. "Shelli says you're high maintenance," he told me. *High maintenance?* I'd barely contacted Irving since our first meeting; we lived and worked on opposite coasts; I made only $50,000 a year. *High maintenance?* That was rich coming from Shelli: she drove a Mercedes, wore designer clothes, and vacationed constantly. It wouldn't have surprised me if she took a private plane to go grocery shopping. I felt frantic and confused. *Why did Azoff screw me like this?*

Peter did nothing to get my money, so I fired him and never spoke to him again. By this point, I was fucking furious. I was also in trouble. I had no savings and, yet again, no job. Sick of dealing with these petty men and their petty games, I decided to take my grievances straight to the top: Bob Morgado.

Bob Morgado was chairman of Warner Music Group and, consequently, Irving Azoff's boss. I couldn't approach him directly, but I knew how to get to him. Morgado was once chief of staff to New York governor Hugh Carey. During Carey's term, he appointed Harold Fisher to head the city's subway system. Harold Fisher's son was a Brooklyn lawyer named Andrew Fisher. I hired Andrew, wrote a letter to Bob Morgado describing everything that had happened, and asked Andrew to take it to him.

Andrew reported back to me: "I spoke to Bob. He doesn't like Irving, and he believes your story, but they won't settle. You'll have to sue to get your money." Andrew said I had a hell of a case, especially given the dirt I had on these men. He almost salivated as he spoke about filing suit. "Time Warner would pay a lot of money to prevent this information from getting out," he said. "You'll be rich." I considered it, and it sounded good. Then Andrew told me the catch: "Just know that if you sue, Morgado says they're going to fire your husband."

I was in an impossible position again. I couldn't afford to get Joey fired. Also, since he had a bigger title and a bigger salary than I did, in my mind, he was more important than me. *How could I bring him down because of my problems?* Looking back, I realize I should have thought of my own career, which was as important as my husband's; I should have stood up regardless of the repercussions against me; I should have had more courage and faith in myself. But I didn't. I decided to protect Joey and didn't sue. Andrew was appalled by the whole ordeal. "These people are despicable," he told me. In fact, they were worse than despicable. They were poisonous. I finally understood Irving's nickname.

Irving's poison worked quickly. Bob Morgado used my letter to bust Irving's balls, and Irving hit the fucking roof. He began bad-mouthing me around the business, calling me a troublemaker, and mocking me for complaining about sexual harassment. He tried to ruin my reputation and make me unemployable in the music business—no one wants to hire a troublemaker, especially not a female one. Now, whenever I ran into friends or acquaintances from the business, they'd say, "What did you do to Irving?" I felt physically sick over it, paralyzed with anger, unable to do anything but cry. The stress became so intense that I began to disassociate from my own feelings. I imagined it all happening to someone else. It was a waking nightmare, and I felt powerless to stop it.

The experience with Irving did have one silver lining: it shook my old worldview, the one that made me blame myself when Ahmet fractured my arm, the one that made me feel guilty for what happened with Jason and Doug. For the first time, I didn't feel guilty. I had an epiphany: *It's not me. These fucking people are crazy.*

Soon after Irving dropped me, I went to Atlantic to see Joey, and he said Doug Morris had heard what happened and wanted me to call him.

"Why would Doug care?" I said.

"It makes no sense," Joey said with a shrug.

For once, my husband and I agreed on something. Given the circumstances, it gave me little comfort. I considered ignoring Doug, but in the end curiosity—and desperation for information—won out. I wasn't going to make it easy on Doug with a phone call, though. I walked right into his office.

"Dorothy!" he said. "What happened?"

"Azoff stopped taking my calls. That's what happened."

"Why would he fire you with a hit record?" Doug asked. In his voice I detected a sense of satisfaction, which I found puzzling. "That's unheard of," he continued. "No one gets fired with a hit record." And then he added something that made so little sense to me, it almost didn't register: "I don't care what Irving thinks you did."

For the next few weeks those words burned in the back of my mind: *I don't care what Irving thinks you did.* What did Irving think I did? All I did was bring him a hit record. I never disrespected him; we never even had a disagreement. What did Doug mean? And then it hit me: *Irving thinks what Doug told him to think.* I knew how fast word traveled between the capos in this business—after all, Doug had found out about my meeting with Tommy Mottola in the time it took me to cross Fifty-Second Street. I also knew Doug and Irving were allies. Maybe Doug was still pissed at the way I left Atlantic. Maybe he didn't want to see me rebound so fast: signing Tara Kemp proved I could succeed without him or Jason Flom. It also proved I could deliver an R&B hit—and I delivered it to another label, no less. I had already seen the way Doug fucked with people behind the scenes with devastating consequences. His demeanor during our meeting gave me the sense that he was fucking with me. To this day, I believe Doug wanted me to read between the lines when he said, "I don't care what Irving thinks you did." He wanted me to know that he had put a bull's-eye on my head and told

Azoff to shoot. He wanted me to understand that no matter where I went or how I succeeded, he could kill my career.

There's a coda to this story: Giant signed Sway and King Tech, the rap duo I found. Their album didn't succeed, but it led them to a radio show on KEML, where Eminem made his broadcast debut. Sway soon became the ubiquitous face of MTV News, and the duo released another album on Interscope in the late 1990s. My eye for talent was vindicated again. Of course, I didn't get anything from the deal. I never even got my final paycheck.

23

SOUTHERN COMFORT

I COULDN'T GET UP. I couldn't move. For two weeks, I didn't shower. I only went outside to walk the dogs. I ate ice cream, if I ate. I spoke to no one. When the phone rang, I stared at it until it fell silent.

After Doug fired me, my first thought was *How do I get a new job?* After Irving fired me, I couldn't think at all. For the first time since my mother's cancer, I stopped worrying about my career. I didn't have a career. I was finished.

I spent all day in bed, crippled by grief. I grieved my lost friends. I grieved my missing purpose. I replayed the hundreds of slights and insults—the ass pinching, the name calling, the tit grabbing, the arm fracturing—and grieved them too.

In this awful pain, I felt the full cost of that childhood message, the one I learned from my mother, my aunts, and Sister Rose Ellen. The cost was this: in a man's world, I had to work twice as hard for half as much. Even then, I was as expendable as a tissue. I could never gain a sure foothold in the corporate world. Raises and promotions went to the harassers, the abusers, and the criminals. People like me hit the glass ceiling and either found a way to accept it or vanished.

About that term, "glass ceiling"—the infamous and unspoken barrier that says to women and minorities, *This is as far as you go*—it had only just come into popular consciousness. The first mainstream mention was in the *Wall Street Journal* in 1986. I don't remember if I had heard it at the time, but I certainly felt it, and I learned something about it that millions before me had learned: they call it glass because it's invisible, not because it's brittle. We all want to believe we'll shatter through it, but in real life, it's hard to even make a dent.

I could have wallowed in my room for months, but the doorbell rang, so I heaved myself out of bed and stumbled toward the door. It was Charlie Minor, looking like a million bucks.

"Girl, you need a shower," he said.

Charlie was an old friend. I'll never forget the first time I met him— it was June 1990, in the Four Seasons Hotel in Boston. I was sitting at the bar drinking a Coke when Charlie walked in. He was of medium height, in good shape, and classically handsome. He wore expensive clothing. I wore a tight red dress that hugged all 105 pounds of me. He didn't know me, but I knew him. He was the executive vice president of A&M Records, and a legendary figure in the promotion business. He also had a great reputation as a ladies' man—girls fell for his southern charm like blossoms from a peach tree. Knowing he wouldn't miss an opportunity to hit on me, I decided to have some fun.

He introduced himself in a lilting southern accent and offered to buy me a drink. As the bartender poured another Coke, Charlie launched into one of the most impressive displays of bullshit I had ever heard. He bragged about how important he was and how much influence he had at A&M. He offered to take me to the annual Kiss 108 radio party, a big concert featuring Bryan Adams and Sting (I didn't tell him I already had tickets with my husband). Then he asked for my room number and suggested we meet there later that night. I looked at him and smiled. He'd bitten the hook. I reached out my hand and stroked his cheek; he took my entire arm and kissed it up and down like Gomez Addams from *The Addams Family*. I could barely keep from laughing. While his lips searched for my neck, Joey came walking toward us.

"Hi, Charlie," Joey said, extending his hand for a shake.

"I'm a little busy," Charlie said. "Let's talk later."

"I see you've met Dorothy," Joey said, about to reel in the catch.

"You know Dorothy?" Charlie said.

"Yeah, she's my wife."

Charlie dropped my arm like it was on fire and yelled at me, "Shame on you, acting like that; you're married!"

"So are you," I said.

After that, we became great friends. I hung out with Charlie whenever I went to L.A., and he found me when he came to New York. I introduced him to Craig Kallman, and the three of us made a team. Charlie knew everyone in the music business and sometimes it seemed like he knew everyone in the world. Coincidentally, Irving hired Charlie as president of Giant Records right after firing me.

Technically, Charlie was in cahoots with my enemy, but as he stood in my doorway trying to cheer me up, I knew he'd always be my friend. Nevertheless, I was in no mood to be cheered up.

"Leave me alone," I told Charlie.

"No way," he said. "I'm taking you out."

"I don't want to go out."

"You're coming with me. We're going to see Irving."

"Irving? I'll wear a red dress to his fucking funeral."

"Are you going to let that little prick beat you?" Charlie asked. He walked past me, went into my bathroom, and turned on the shower.

"Get in," he said.

As the hot water ran over me, Charlie's words rang in my head. *Are you going to let that little prick beat you?* I started feeling better. After I got out of the shower, I slipped into my bedroom to get dressed and found that Charlie had laid out an entire outfit for me, including shoes and a matching bra and panties. In that moment, I couldn't have loved him more. He cared, and he wasn't afraid to show it. He stood up for me at the lowest point of my life, when no one else was there. I heard him holler, "Put on some makeup," and I knew that Charlie was my true friend.

We went to a club where Irving held court. Irving saw me and waved like nothing had happened. I wanted to crack him in the face, but I just waved back. I'd been having a hard time controlling my anger for a while now—my husband's left eye could attest to that—but I didn't know how else to react. It was exhausting being in my own head. I don't know what I would have done if Charlie hadn't stayed by my side the whole night. It took balls, doing that in front of his boss.

I'd later learn of Charlie's infamous reputation as a wild man who cavorted with prostitutes and strippers, but that wasn't the Charlie I knew. To me, he was one of the only trustworthy men in the business. I told him my deepest feelings and darkest secrets—how I felt betrayed and abandoned by Jason, Doug, and Joey; how, at home, I felt the walls closing in on me; how much I hated Irving for firing me the way he did. Charlie never betrayed me or used this information against me. He had the gift of empathy. Even though he was going through a messy divorce himself—it seemed his hair had turned gray overnight—he made space for me. He listened to my troubles and gave me sound advice on my marriage: divorce that lying, cheating dog, he said. I had considered it, but I still felt too guilty and too proud to admit defeat.

Charlie's kindness helped me regain my composure. I climbed out of my hole and began looking for a new job. When I heard through the grapevine that RCA had just hired a new president and was looking for A&R executives, I had the guts to put myself back in the game. To this day, I thank Charlie Minor for that.

24

TOO SHORT

RCA's NEW VICE PRESIDENT OF A&R was Ric Aliberte, brother of Frannie Aliberte, the number two man at WEA. The Aliberte brothers were from Boston, like my husband, and I knew Frannie from my days at Atlantic. He had a reputation for being a straight arrow. I asked him to speak to Ric for me, and he threw me a break because he knew Irving had fucked me over.

"I'll do it," Frannie said, "but I'm warning you: Ric is nothing like me."

It felt good to be able to call in a favor from a top executive—it meant I didn't have to walk in off the street as just another stranger looking for a break. It was an advantage I had earned through years of hard work.

I had to wait two weeks to see Ric, so I figured I'd gain another advantage by using the old trick that had helped me get my job at Atlantic—I invited Ric's assistant to lunch. We met at a restaurant near the RCA offices on Sixth Avenue and hit it off immediately. She gave me the scoop on the team at RCA: the previous VP of A&R, Jeff Aldrich, had just been fired for sexually harassing a female subordinate. Ric had a background in management, but he came in with no prior experience working at a label. Ric's lack of experience didn't worry me; I liked how he got the job and what it said about RCA. Here was a company that actually fired people for sexual harassment.

When I met Ric for my interview, he was smoking a cigarette. He was overweight and he cursed. Frannie was right: Ric was nothing like him. Our interview was short. Ric said I could have the job, but first I had to meet RCA president Joe Galante and get his approval.

Joe Galante was the former president of RCA's Country Music Division in Nashville. He was a rare specimen: an Italian good old boy. When he first arrived in Nashville, no one liked him. He was a New Yorker, a numbers man, and a pencil pusher. He rose to his position from the marketing side of the business, not the artistic side. There was a joke around Nashville that went, "What has two arms, two legs, and no ears?" The answer, of course: Joe Galante. Even though he didn't have an ear for music, Joe turned RCA into the number one country label, a position it held for a decade.

Joe seemed just fine to me. His years in Nashville had kept him apart from the New York music establishment, which meant I didn't have to worry about Doug's machinations. Plus, RCA was not a major player in the business. It was run by BMG, a group of Germans who were even further removed from the New York scene than Joe was. I felt like I was applying for the witness protection program.

Our meeting was short and direct. He told me he liked the Tara Kemp record and offered me the job. Later, I found out that Ric's assistant had had a role in my hiring. Whenever another A&R person called to apply for the job, she threw out the message. She wanted me to get it, and she worked behind the scenes to make sure I did. My strategy had paid off again.

I joined RCA in late March 1991 to find the A&R Department in a mess. They say in life that showing up is 90 percent of the battle. Ric missed that memo. During my first week, he only came in once. Without anyone directing A&R, it was hard to know what to do. The following week, Ric barely showed up again. He'd call the office and say he was having a root canal at Dr. Tischler's office in Woodstock, New York, where he lived. At first we all felt sorry for him—no one enjoys a root canal—but as the weeks went on, Ric's absence continued, and every day, he'd call in with the same excuse: "I'm getting a root canal." *Come on, Ric, the human body only has thirty-two teeth.* Soon, I dubbed him "Tisch."

For reasons I still don't understand, Joe gave Ric a seemingly endless supply of slack. At first, Joe acted surprised when he made his rounds of the RCA offices and found out that Ric hadn't shown up. I felt that this act was for my benefit. Joe wasn't an idiot. He must have seen through Ric's excuses—one day he asked me, "How long did it take you to figure it out?"

"Two weeks," I said.

In Ric's absence, Joe began piling extra work on me. I was in the studio editing radio mixes, setting up remixes for dance music, approving band budgets, and always covering for Ric's absence. I lied to all the managers about their projects. After a while, I was handling most of Ric's job without Ric's title or salary.

Joe grew more furious by the day, and he let me know it, sometimes by yelling, but mostly by drowning me in paperwork. Unlike Doug Morris, who kept the business in his head, Joe needed a memo for everything. I never saw so much paper in my life. Every day, I'd arrive to find my inbox stuffed full of notes. Joe loved meetings, too. He would have a meeting just to discuss having another meeting.

His behavior began raising familiar red flags. For instance, he seemed more comfortable dealing with male executives, and he had hired only two female department heads. They headed low-level departments: Press and Art. Typical.

In A&R, Joe tried to run the department by committee. If we wanted to sign an act, he'd play it for every department head, as well as for other staff members who had nothing to do with A&R, and ask everyone's opinion. It was obvious he did not trust his A&R staff, and this made our work twice as hard. You can't do A&R by committee, in the same way that you can't make art by committee.

Perhaps there was something to that old Nashville joke. Joe had no ears. He was a businessman, not an artist. At the time, Nabisco was running an ad campaign for a new line of snacks, and Joe told us to follow their example. *What the fuck does Nabisco have to do with music?* I thought. I wasn't in a position to say this, of course, and no one in Joe's inner circle had the guts to say it. They were all yes-men, and Joe dragged them around like a security blanket.

The biggest red flag, though, was the way Joe darted around the office shouting out orders like Yosemite Sam. He stood the same height as Irving Azoff, and like Irving, he seemed to hold it against the entire world. I gave Joe a nickname that I used whenever he got on my nerves: Too Short.

Despite these misgivings, however, I liked Joe. I wanted to do well for him. I appreciated him giving me another chance at my dream job, and I felt loyal to him for saving me from the sting of the Poison Dwarf.

In fact, Azoff's poison still hadn't left my system. On my birthday in April 1991, Charlie sent me a huge bouquet of flowers. He called later that day and said, "I put those flowers on my expenses. When Irving saw it, he yelled, 'I'm not paying for Dorothy Carvello's flowers! She's a cunt!'" Charlie and I had a good laugh. It felt good to get under Irving's skin, but I had bigger plans for him.

After Irving fired me, he offered Craig a label deal for all of Big Beat Records. Giant had only signed an artist deal with Tara Kemp, and Irving was no fool—he knew Craig's value, and he wanted to snatch him up while he still could. I intended to make sure Craig rejected Irving's offer. I couldn't let Irving win this one, not after what he did to me. I came up with a plan to steer Craig to Doug Morris. The way I rationalized it, Doug was the lesser of two evils.

Joey and I took Craig to dinner, and I made my case: "You can't go with Irving," I said. "He fucks everybody. Look at how he fucked me. He'll do the same to you. Let Joey introduce you to Doug Morris."

Everything went according to plan. Craig was like catnip to Doug: Jewish, Ivy League educated, and talented. I had just introduced Doug to a new and improved Jason Flom. In June 1991, Craig took a position as an executive vice president at Atlantic. To thank me, he paid for a vacation to Florida that Joey and I had been planning. It was a kind and generous gesture. I don't know what Irving thought of all this, or if he even knew my role in making sure he lost Craig, but I had my revenge. That was enough.

25

A GOOD MAN IS HARD TO FIND

My first week at RCA, I met Senior Vice President McDreamy. Randy Goodman had the classically handsome features of a Hollywood movie star. He dressed well, like he had just stepped out of a Brooks Brothers catalog. His hair was perfectly cut to accent his face, he wore glasses, and he seemed to give off an aura of light. He was the senior VP of marketing, and he was Joe's right-hand man. I rarely saw one of them without the other. When Randy first came into my office, I thought, *Oh shit, this could be a problem.* When he told me his name, I smiled like a schoolgirl. *Randy . . . how appropriate.*

Randy functioned as the general manager of RCA, even though Joe didn't give him the money or the title. He was involved in every aspect of product development, which meant I saw him every day. I got used to the daily adrenaline rush when I heard him coming down the hall, got used to my temperature rising when he appeared in my doorway. Sometimes Randy and I just stared at each other, sizing each other up like animals in a zoo. After he'd leave my office, I'd run to the secretaries to talk about how handsome he was. I was in serious trouble.

From the beginning, Randy fascinated me. We had a natural rapport, which I used to my advantage. For example, I pretended I didn't know what price positioning was just so he could explain it to me, which he did with customary patience.

Randy was married too, but he wasn't dead. He flirted with me as much as I flirted with him, the sexual tension flowing thick like honey. I knew it was wrong to daydream about banging him, but I couldn't help myself. Coworkers began making fun of me for being so obviously attracted to him, and all I could do was smile and nod.

At the same time, I sensed something different about Randy, something that went beyond Ahmet's philosophy of do whatever you want, whenever you want, wherever you want, with whomever you want. Randy radiated something pure and decent, something I wasn't used to feeling from a man in the music business. He was the first man in my experience who said please and thank you—with Ahmet and Doug, it was just, "Get me this, get me that." He was the first man who seemed secure in the presence of a strong, smart woman. He didn't dumb himself down for me, and he didn't expect me to dumb myself down for him.

In fact, Randy was the opposite of Ahmet in nearly every way. He was the opposite of me in many ways, too. He was refined, and he never cursed or lost his temper. I felt feral in comparison. For me, the word "fuck" was a verb, noun, adjective, and anything else I needed it to be. I wanted to learn from Randy, and he had a natural teaching ability, but from the start, I invested too much of myself in him.

There's a term for the relationship that formed between us: "work spouse." It's a common relationship, and an easy one to fall into. When you spend eight to ten hours a day with a man and travel with him for work, you naturally form an emotional bond, often sharing moments and feelings that aren't appropriate between coworkers. I had gone down this path with Jason and Craig, but I didn't have a sexual attraction toward them. That's part of what made Randy so unprecedented in my career.

As for Randy's thoughts, I can't say. He was too much of a gentleman to reveal them. I don't know if he saw me as his work wife the way I saw him as my work husband—all I can say is, when he brought his real wife into the office, he didn't introduce us. For my part, I felt guilty about wanting to cheat, but only because I knew it was wrong as a general principle. The only thing stopping me from banging Randy Goodman was Randy Goodman.

Joe treated Randy like his golden boy. Whenever Randy and I were alone, Joe appeared out of thin air and found some excuse to take Randy away. Many times, I asked Joe to transfer me to marketing—Randy's department—and every time, he walked out of my office in disgust.

I felt that Joe wanted to get rid of me. I had been at RCA for only a few months when he tried to foist me on Joel Katz and Don Perry at Kane Records. I knew of Joel Katz—he was Charlie Minor's attorney (I always laughed at how Charlie, with his southern accent, pronounced it "Jo-elle")—but I wanted nothing to do with music-business attorneys after the Peter Lopez debacle. Also, Joe Galante was a longtime client of Joel's, and many on the RCA staff were also his clients. Joe even gave Joel the label/production deal that turned into Kane Records.

Joel Katz was based in Atlanta, a hotbed of talent at the time. He represented L.A. Reid, Babyface, Jimmy Jam, Terry Lewis, and Dallas Austin (years later, when Dallas Austin was arrested in Dubai and sentenced to four years in prison for bringing cocaine into the country, Joel spent ten days in Dubai and worked with Senator Orrin Hatch to secure his release). Joel also represented country legends like Willie Nelson and George Strait, and he did them a great service—most labels paid country and R&B acts a lower royalty rate than pop acts. Joel Katz changed that for country artists.

Joel dominated the legal side of the business. He put his longtime partner, friend, confidant, and problem solver, Don Perry, in charge of the artists. Don was Joel's sidekick. If you wanted to get to Joel, you had to get through Don. If you wanted to get to both of them, you had to cough up a fat fee. Unlike Joe Galante, these guys had street smarts. I had street smarts, too, but they weren't enough to put me on the level of Joel Katz and Don Perry.

Joe Galante set up a meeting for me in Atlanta toward the end of 1991, and Joel Katz showed up dressed head to toe in lavish designer clothing. He was always the best-dressed man in the music business. He said that only the elite worked for him, and I guessed that excluded me. He didn't make an offer, and I returned to RCA, where Too Short was cold and condescending, Tisch rarely came to work, and my only reason for sticking around was Randy Goodman.

Joe, Ric, and Randy reminded me of the Atlantic triptych of Ahmet, Doug, and Jason, but the situation was even more unbearable. Joe was a narcissist like Ahmet, but he wasn't fun like Ahmet. He was demanding, distrustful, detached, and passive-aggressive. I never felt secure. He told me I was doing well, but he didn't act like he meant it. No one but Randy Goodman was good enough for him, and he even treated Randy like shit. I saw anxiety on Randy's face daily. Joe tried to control our every action. He wanted us to be robots, automatons, copies of him—and yet, he didn't even meet his own expectations. If he had to work for himself, he would be fired.

Joe and Doug had much in common. Both were cunning, both were condescending, both were adept at the art of the mind fuck, and both knew how to work their company systems to benefit themselves. Joe took nepotism to a new level at RCA, in violation of BMG's strict corporate policies. His sister-in-law worked for the company. She was nice, but we all had to kiss her ass because she acted as his spy. His daughter worked at BMG. His ex-wife, Georgeann, managed artists on the RCA country label, and his third wife had been a product manager at Arista, RCA's sister label. I was also suspicious of the Nashville travel agency Joe made us use—they'd give him all the details whenever we traveled, allowing him to keep an eye on us at all times. I knew many people in Nashville from my days traveling with Ahmet, but I didn't trust Joe with that information.

Another thing Joe and Doug had in common—along with every other man I worked for—was their love of petty gossip. One day I went to visit my husband at Atlantic, and Doug invited me to his office. He wanted dirt on Joe. "I heard he was a country bumpkin," Doug said. I didn't respond. I knew Doug didn't understand country music. Back when I worked for him, I often suggested that we use some of our country acts as songwriters for our pop acts. Doug always said the same thing: "Sweetheart, don't worry about those people." Whatever problems I had with Joe, I knew he was a pioneer in country music. He signed Alabama—an act Doug had tried and failed to sign. He signed Clint Black. He worked with Dolly Parton, the Judds, Ronnie Milsap, Lorrie

Morgan, Martina McBride, and so many others, helping to build them into stadium acts. But the heads of the New York record companies didn't let Joe into their little cabal. He was too New York for Nashville and too Nashville for New York.

Increasingly, I found myself the target of Joe's anger. Part of this was my fault—I still did business the Ahmet Ertegun way and didn't fully grasp how my behavior came across in a normal business setting. Randy tried to teach me, but old habits die hard. For example, at one conference in Atlanta, Randy gave a speech, and I sat in the back of the room watching. When he finished, I let out a piercing, two-fingers-in-the-mouth, Brooklyn-schoolyard-style whistle. Joe spun his head around like Linda Blair in *The Exorcist* to see who it was. He leveled me with a look like he was about to brand my ass with the scarlet letter—A, for Ahmet and Atlantic.

Another time, in preparation for a corporate retreat, Joe sent a memo around saying those below the title of VP had to share a room to save money. Joe was famously stingy with his workers, and infamously liberal with his artists—he paid $30 million for ZZ Top, an aging act with no hits on the horizon, but God forbid his employees waste a dollar on their comfort. Joe wanted us to write our choice of roommate on the memo, so I wrote Randy Goodman's name on it in capital letters. I thought it was funny. I knew Ahmet would have loved it. Joe, on the other hand, returned the memo to me. At the top, in big black letters, he wrote, "NOT FUNNY."

Male executives, such as Ric Aliberte, received different treatment. At the time, Ric lived in Woodstock, a hundred miles away from the RCA office. Joe rented him an apartment closer to the city, with the understanding that Ric would eventually move permanently. Instead, Ric bought a new house in Woodstock and used the company car service for the two-hour ride back home. Jack Carden, the financial guy at RCA, wore the carpet out to Ric's office crying about the bills—one was $13,000 for a month's worth of car service. Ric didn't give a shit, and Joe let him get away with it over and over again.

It was not as if Ric was raking in the hits. The A&R Department under his watch was like a five-alarm fire, and instead of putting it out, Ric threw gallons of gasoline on it while Joe gave him more and more money to keep the fire blazing. Even when Ric finally committed an unpardonable offense, Joe didn't fire him. Instead, he began looking for someone to hire over Ric—a senior vice president of A&R.

One day I got called into Joe's office. I hated going to Joe's office—it was ugly, and it usually contained Joe—but he was the boss, and I had no choice. I went. As soon as I entered, I noticed Joe's face was red with anger. He raised his voice to me. Apparently, Joe had received a call from Joe Eisenstein, the senior VP of human resources at BMG. Eisenstein alerted Joe that Ric had authorized an unexplained $2,500 cash advance, and it was rumored to be for an employee's breast enhancement surgery. Joe waved the paperwork at me and told me to look at it. I had heard something about the surgery months ago, but it didn't affect me, so I forgot it.

"Joe, I had nothing to do with this," I said. "That's not my signature. I'm not a VP, so I can't sign for a cash advance." I was confused. Why was Joe talking to me about this and not the VP of the A&R Department? I felt embarrassed and somehow degraded, as if the only reason I had to listen to this harangue was that I was the only woman in the A&R Department.

Joe's anger abated into introspection. "I'm not a bad person," he said. "If someone needs surgery, I'll help them. But not for tits." Then his anger swelled again. "As far as I'm concerned," he spat, "they aren't big enough for the trouble."

I shuddered inwardly. The whole situation was fucked up—Joe should have never had this conversation with me. I was angry that he did. I should have approached Joe Eisenstein at BMG personnel, gotten Joe Galante fired, and left with a fat check. But like with Ahmet, Doug, and Irving, I wanted Joe's approval, so I said nothing.

Same mistake, different man.

26

MR. FREEZE

In mid-1992, Joe called a meeting in the conference room with me and the other A&R executives in New York, along with Bennett Kaufman from California via telephone. Ric came to the meeting four hours late. He made an excuse, as usual. "I just got back from Chicago," he said. "I was up all night with Prince listening to some new music he's going to give to RCA." Judging by the looks of him, he wasn't lying about staying up all night. As for the rest, the phone line crackled, and Bennett Kaufman said he had seen Prince out at dinner in Los Angeles that very same night.

I knew Ric was full of shit—we all did—but I would never embarrass a colleague like that. It served no purpose. Joe sat speechless. He'd been quietly planning to replace Ric since the boob-job debacle, but his plan didn't stay quiet for long. There was a mole in the room.

A few weeks later, *Spy* magazine ran a brutal article tearing RCA and Joe to shreds and citing specific events from the meeting. It was so bad that Joe forbade us to have the magazine in the offices. I walked several blocks to buy it and read it on the street. As I stood outside devouring the article, I knew everyone in the industry was doing the same in boardrooms, offices, conference rooms, and company cars. The incestuous music business loved nothing more than gossip, and this was devastating gossip.

The article is worth quoting at length, because it shows where RCA, Joe Galante, and our A&R Department stood in the eyes of our peers (if they even considered us peers):

> [RCA] can no longer be recognized as one of its own species. These days, when RCA seldom has an entry on the pop charts, when some of its most promising artists are trying to break their contracts, it's nearly impossible to believe that in the 1950s, RCA was an undisputed industry leader.

This was a hard truth. RCA once boasted Elvis, Sam Cooke, and Dolly Parton, among many others. The legendary RCA Studio B was home to some of the most famous recordings in history—it is now on the National Register of Historic Places. And yet, the only thing we had going for us at the moment was the occasional catalog reissue and hits from Bruce Hornsby and the *Dirty Dancing* soundtrack.

We should have been on top of the world. We had a full cross-country promotion staff, including Butch Waugh, senior VP of promotion; Kenny Ortiz and Skip Miller in R&B; Deborah Radel in publicity; Ron Urban in finance; Roger Skelton and Jim Cooperman in business affairs; Bruce Flohr and Greg Linn in marketing; and Terry Anzaldo and Lou Simon in promotion. Ron Fair, one of the best A&R execs in the business, worked on the West Coast. This was the most talented group of people at any label I had ever worked with. I couldn't understand why we weren't hotter, until I realized that between Ric's constant absence and Joe's distrust of his own A&R Department, we had no morale. No morale meant no hits. No hits meant no credibility with radio stations. No credibility with radio stations meant no big acts, which meant no hits, which meant no morale. It was a vicious cycle.

It was Joe's doing. He demoralized us. Where Doug had a gift for making you feel great while he fucked you over, Joe just fucked you over. Sometimes I thought he wanted us to feel like shit, even to believe we were shit. He lacked the gift of inspiration. Every time he'd take us on another pointless retreat, I'd ask Ric why he didn't take us to Graceland, home of RCA's patron saint, Elvis Presley. Even Ahmet, who had nothing to do with Elvis, would call ahead and close Graceland for his executives and artists. For Ahmet, it was a ritual, a sacrifice to the King of Rock 'n' Roll. Ahmet would smoke a joint and ask the King to watch over us. This simple gesture meant the world to us. It gave us a bar to reach, a prize to chase.

Joe apparently didn't see the point. He could have inspired us right there in the RCA building. Mike Moran, Elvis's recording engineer, still worked in the RCA studio (his wife, Linda Moran, typed up my infamous memo at Atlantic). Many days, I would find a quiet moment and seek Mike out in the studio or sit down next to him in the cafeteria and ask him about Elvis and the old days.

We also had access to the audio engineers who recorded classics by Perry Como, Dolly Parton, and David Bowie. Joe didn't take advantage of any of it. He failed to inspire us, and he failed to hire a head of A&R who could inspire us—as the *Spy* article noted, "At RCA, being the head of A&R could have you pining for a position with job security—say, manager of the Yankees. Over the last two years, the job has been handled by four different executives. A tale circulated about one of [the executives] crystallizes the problem: The executive was said to have shown up four hours late for a scheduled A&R conference call, offering the excuse that he had been up late with Prince the night before. 'Prince?' a voice on the L.A. side of the call said skeptically. 'Gee, I saw him having dinner at Carlos 'N Charlie's last night.'"

Everyone knew that last bit was about Ric. What Joe didn't want anyone to know—and what the *Spy* article made very clear—was that RCA had to hire a headhunter to fill the job. This was pathetic and emasculating for Joe, especially because it wasn't entirely his choice. Again, from the *Spy* article: "The depth of RCA's troubles may best be measured by its difficulties in finding someone to take the A&R job. In an industry where connections and word of mouth are everything and where upper-level executive slots never get advertised, RCA had to hire a headhunter to find someone. That decision was apparently made by Michael Dornemann, the German head of Bertelsmann Music Group (not by Galante), in a kind of second-guessing that has been standard procedure at RCA since its sale."

This was brutal stuff—all of Joe's shortcomings (no pun intended) were on display. RCA was circling the drain on his watch, and now everyone in the business knew it. Everyone knew that no one wanted to work for him, that he was an incompetent leader who couldn't even make his own decisions. *Spy* magazine did to Joe's reputation what Brutus did to Caesar.

The article made one last fatal thrust, quoting an unnamed "artist manager" who said, "When you deal with Tommy Mottola at Sony or Lenny Warokner at Warner Bros., you know you're dealing with guys who have the power to make decisions. . . . You don't get that feeling talking to Galante."

I felt bad for Joe. Every word of that article rang true, but I still felt loyal to the man who had rescued me with a job when I thought my career was over, despite how poorly he treated me at that job. I had no such feelings, however, for the new head of A&R, Dave Novik.

The headhunter had to scrape the bottom of the barrel to find Dave Novik. His hiring was a perfect example of solving a problem by creating an even bigger problem. I was familiar with this move— sadly, it was how I conducted much of my personal life. Dave Novik came from Columbia Records. Donnie Ienner had just fired him. I wondered if Joe ever called Donnie to get the scoop on Dave. If he didn't, he should have.

When I met Dave, it was hate at first sight. As far as I was concerned, everything was wrong with him—the way he talked, the way he walked, even the way he looked. He always had a dumb expression on his face, like if you asked him his name, he'd be pressed to come up with an answer. I called him "Mr. Freeze," after the Batman villain. He seemed to spread an icy chill everywhere he went. He was cold, and A&R people don't like cold. Cold means failure in a job where success comes in hot streaks. Every failed record, every stiff, brought the fear— the gut-quivering fear—that the final cold spell had set in and the hits had dried up for good. When Dave Novik came in, I felt cold to my marrow. I knew my days at RCA were numbered.

Soon after Dave came on board, I sent an assistant into his office to toss the place for anything interesting. She came back with a paper with all the A&R staff names on it. At the top of the paper was a title: "Personality Profiles." Then, it read:

Mark—Mickey Eichner's Son
Ric—Producer, VP
Dorothy—Unrelenting

This must have been a cheat sheet for Dave to get to know his new employees by reputation. I should have taken this list to Human Resources. BMG had a strict Personnel Department, and they would have fired Dave in a second. I didn't do it because, again, I felt loyal to Joe. He had lost his first A&R head, Jeff Aldrich, to sexual harassment. Ric was not department head material, so he was gone too. Joe needed someone to do the job, and he picked Dave. Again, I sacrificed myself for a man's sake. Again, I would live to regret it.

27

WITH A LITTLE HELP FROM MY FRIENDS

In the summer of 1992, I signed a label deal with ID Records in Chicago. Owned by Steve "Silk" Hurley, a prominent DJ and remixer, and his partner, Frank Rodrigo, ID was primarily a dance label with crossover appeal. RCA paid $300,000 for a stake in the label, giving us the first choice of any acts Silk signed along with access to his remixing and production skills. I was particularly excited about one of his acts—Chantay Savage. It was the first major deal I landed for RCA, and I believed it had the potential to grow into a lucrative partnership.

Before the ink could dry on the deal, however, Dave Novik began meddling with it. He traveled to Chicago with Joe to see Silk. After that trip, I found myself relegated to the sidelines as the deal was restructured for substantially more money than I had negotiated. I don't know why Joe and Dave decided to throw so much more money at ID, and I never had a chance to find out. Silk asked Joe to take the project away from me and transfer it to Skip Miller, the senior VP of R&B. Joe didn't stick up for me.

Skip was a regal man—tall, handsome, and always well dressed. He thought what Joe, Dave, and Silk had done to me was unfair, and he invited me to dinner to talk about it. We ended up having Sunday dinner at my place, and as we ate, Skip expressed his sympathy. He knew

Dave wanted to get rid of me, so he offered to keep me on his budget. He thought I had talent, and he wanted to work with me. He said he'd speak with Joe about it. I was touched—Skip didn't have to stick up for me, but he was one of the few men who did.

Unfortunately, there was only so much he could do. A week later, he called and told me Joe wouldn't authorize his idea. I appreciated Skip going to bat for me, and I still do, but I was upset. I realized I was dealing with the same man over and over again in my career. Sometimes he was shorter, sometimes taller, sometimes thinner, sometimes fatter, but he was always the same man. I didn't yet have the wisdom to understand the ways I sought this man out—the ways I attracted narcissists, assholes, and addicts, as much as they attracted me—but I was tired of making the same choices and getting the same results. My career felt like a merry-go-round. Find a job. Sign an act. Become marginalized. Get no credit for success. Get fired. Repeat. I felt vindicated when Chantay Savage's single went gold, but I was on the "get no credit for success" part of the merry-go-round.

My descent into hell had begun, and Dave Novik acted as my tour guide. This was the man who branded me "unrelenting" before he even met me. Now he rarely spoke to me except to second-guess me, or to make me second-guess myself. He gave me the worst jobs—there was no shortage of shit jobs at RCA—and he never invited me to A&R showcases. He was mean and petty. Joe kissed his ass constantly, and I lost respect for Joe. I had no respect to lose for Dave.

Under Dave Novik, time seemed to stretch on endlessly. Every day felt like a week. I slogged through work only to return home and struggle with my husband. Randy became my reason for showing up every morning. He was the only one who seemed to care. He'd come into my office and offer advice, counsel, and an open ear for my troubles. He was slowly molding me into a better A&R executive. Unfortunately, the sexual tension between us was part of the problem, but I was in denial about it, and I couldn't talk to him about it. Thankfully, whenever the pressure became too much to bear, I had escapes.

On the West Coast, I had my good friend Charlie Minor. Whenever I visited L.A., he'd meet me with a kiss on the forehead, a big hug, and an assurance that everything would be OK. We'd vent about how no one understood us and how everyone demanded too much from us. We never talked about his many girlfriends, but he continued to give me relationship advice. I told him my husband thought our relationship was improper. Charlie laughed hard about that one. Every time Charlie and I parted, we said, "I love you." This was new to me. I always had a hard time saying those words, but with Charlie, it was easy. Rarely does platonic love exist between a man and a woman, but it existed between Charlie and me. I didn't have to worry about pleasing or disappointing him. I could just be myself; that was enough. When we spent time together, I didn't feel alone like I did everywhere else. I felt understood.

On the East Coast, I had Frank DiLeo. I first met Frank in 1990, but I knew him by reputation long before that. Frank was famous for managing Michael Jackson, although he'd been fired in 1989 under mysterious circumstances. Frank landed on his feet, becoming a movie star in *Goodfellas*, playing Paul Sorvino's brother, Tuddy. He had recently returned to New York City and opened a management company for artists, producers, and writers (Richie Sambora and Taylor Dayne were clients). I was interested in one of his acts—Renee Props, a soap-opera star who wanted to become a singer—and I went to hear her demo tape at Frank's headquarters. The headquarters took up an entire floor of a building on West Fifty-Seventh Street. Frank's assistant escorted me into his office, where I saw a five-foot-two Italian guy chomping on a cigar, sitting next to a baby grand piano. I bent over to shake his hand, and he said, "Why are you wearing a red bra?" I replied, "Why are you looking down my shirt?" We both laughed. It was the beginning of a beautiful friendship.

By the fall of 1992—not long after he had landed the role of Frankie "Mr. Big" Sharp in *Wayne's World*—I started hanging with Frank six nights a week. I saw him more than I saw my own husband. It helped that Frank was always available. He was married but didn't live with his wife (I called her the Invisible Woman). Every morning on my walk to work, I passed Frank's apartment building, which served breakfast on the ground floor. Most days I'd stop in and eat with him before work. After work, I usually met him for dinner. At the time, Trattoria Dell'Arte on Seventh Avenue was the hot restaurant in New York, so that's where we went—Frank had to have the best of everything. I loved how people in the restaurant lined up to pay their respects, just like in *Goodfellas*. He truly lived the part.

At these dinners we gossiped about everyone in the music business. Frank bitched about his lawyer—Joel Katz, whom I knew. I bitched about my boss—Joe Galante, whom he knew. He had once worked for RCA, and he laughed when I talked about becoming a top-level executive there. "Nothing's gonna happen for you at RCA," he said. "Those guys, they're from Nashville. You're not their type of girl. You're my type of girl. You're a broad." Part of me knew he was right, but I didn't want to believe him.

Frank and I each had childhood nicknames (Bebe and Tookie), but we gave each other new nicknames. I dubbed him the King, and he called me Virginia, after Bugsy Siegel's mistress, Virginia Hill—the ultimate Mob moll. This renaming was a unique expression of intimacy, a sort of christening into friendship.

Like Charlie, Frank was wildly generous. He'd call me and say, "Virginia, I'm flying to L.A.—come." He'd upgrade me to first class on the flight, then drive me to the Four Seasons Hotel, get out of his car, and hand hundred-dollar bills to the bellhops, saying, "Take care of her." Then he'd motor to his cabana at the Peninsula Hotel, where the West Coast music industry flocked to party with him. He'd chomp on his cigar and regale us with tales of *Goodfellas*. If he was in the mood, he'd talk about Michael Jackson and his pet chimp, Bubbles. Michael took Bubbles everywhere, and Frank often had to change Bubbles's diaper—he bragged that he could do it in less than three minutes. Once, on tour in Hong Kong, Michael insisted that Bubbles have his own hotel suite, so Frank had to set it up and deal with the damages after the chimp destroyed the room.

Sometimes, I was able to return Frank's generosity. One day at RCA, he called and said, "Virginia, I need you to get Richie Sambora's parents tickets to see Tony Bennett at Radio City Music Hall." I asked my secretary to place a call for me to Columbia Records, and I got the tickets. Then, without really thinking, I said to the secretaries in the pit, "Richie has the biggest dick in the music business." They asked how I knew, and I told them about the time I was backstage with Skid Row on the Bon Jovi tour and I accidentally saw Richie coming out of the shower. "The guys in the band call it the Monument, after the Washington Monument," I said. "It arrives an hour before he does." I was daydreaming again.

Frank led a wild life, but he went to Catholic Mass every Sunday. If I happened to be with him on a Sunday, no matter where we were in the world, I had to attend. Refusal was not an option. He was a strict Catholic in church, but when it came to morality in the real world, he wasn't so different from Ahmet. Maybe that's why I liked him.

The adventures I had with Frank are still among the most memorable of my life, but after a while, I realized I was using these adventures to escape reality. In a way, we both were. We were adrift, looking for the next thing to come along. Frank was deeply hurt when Michael Jackson fired him, and he hoped to get back into the King of Pop's good graces. I was hiding from the pain of a failed marriage and a job I increasingly hated. He provided a wonderful distraction, allowing me to delay the difficult decisions I needed to make in my life, but I couldn't delay them forever.

28

KNIGHT IN SHINING ARMOR

By Christmastime 1992, Dave Novik had completely sucked the joy out of my work. With Joe's blessing, he created a hostile work environment for me. Joe allowed a culture of toxic masculinity at RCA. I felt I was not welcome anywhere. I aired my grievances to Randy—I told him over and over again that Joe and Dave were gunning for me, that I didn't feel safe in my job. He listened and somehow made sure I did not get fired, at least not that week. The next week, he'd do it again. I cast him in the role of Knight in Shining Armor, always saving me, the Damsel in Distress.

Randy continued guiding me. In meetings, I usually just blurted out my opinion. Whenever I blurted, Randy made a face like I shouldn't have said what I did. After the meeting, he'd come to my office and explain to me that I could make my point if I chose my words more wisely. I never felt offended by his suggestions—quite the opposite, I found them clear and beneficial.

My admiration and respect for him grew daily, but I couldn't express it in a proper and mature way. Whenever Randy spoke at one of Joe's worthless meetings, I'd just sit there and gaze at him, as little hearts and rainbows and unicorns danced around his head. If other executives didn't pay complete attention to what he was saying, I'd feel personally offended. The sexual tension between us was still overt and obvious. I remember standing outside my office one day, talking to Randy, while Ric looked on (there must have been a full moon, because Ric showed up to work). I didn't notice Ric standing near us until Randy left and the rest of the world came back into focus.

"You two should get a room," Ric said.

"Ric, it's not for lack of trying."

My feelings for Randy were a jumble. I admired him; I respected him; I didn't know how to act around him; I wanted to bang him. It was confusing. When the sexual tension became too awkward for me, I visited my old mentor. I knew Ahmet would tell me what to do.

It still felt strange to enter 75 Rockefeller Plaza and take the elevator to the second floor. There had been too much rough water recently, and not enough of it had gone under the bridge. But I always felt welcome with Ahmet. Every time I visited, he greeted me with two open arms, two kisses on the cheek, and that frog croak voice: "Sit down."

I explained my dilemma with Randy, and as usual, Ahmet told me the opposite of what I needed to hear. "What's the problem?" he said, brushing aside my moral qualms. "If you want to fuck him, fuck him. Just don't fuck up your marriage." (Keep in mind, my husband's office was thirty feet away from Ahmet's, but that didn't register to me or Ahmet). He told me that once we fucked the sexual tension would go away. It made sense.

As the holiday break approached, I felt exhausted. I was tired of the tension with Randy—Ahmet's advice had left me more conflicted than ever. I was tired of Joe's severity—at the company Christmas party, I let out a loud laugh at a joke that Ric told, and Joe yelled at me for laughing. Most of all, I was tired of Dave Novik's bullshit—his secretary told me that he was going to fire me over the break. I had no contract at RCA, and that meant I wouldn't get a severance package if I lost my job. Every time I saw Dave lurching around the office, I pictured him as Ebenezer Scrooge, throwing me out on my ass just in time for Christmas.

These men were killing my spirit. Everything they did seemed designed to make me lose my self-esteem. For the first time, I started questioning my talent. I felt like I was going deaf—not literally, but as an A&R executive, I had a hard time *hearing*. I found it harder and harder to trust my own intuition, my own taste, and my own ears.

Again, I turned to Randy. I told him what I had heard from Dave's secretary—the most insulting part was that Dave apparently intended to fire me over the phone. Randy assured me that I wouldn't lose my job. Just to be safe, I shut off my answering machine during the break. If Dave wanted to fire me, he would have to face me.

After the holiday, Dave didn't say a word to me. In early 1993, he and Joe promoted me to associate director, giving me a $15,000 raise and a contract. The title was bogus, but at least the contract gave me security if they fired me. I was sure I had Randy Goodman to thank for it. When I got the promotion and raise, I thought, *Finally, these assholes are going to give me a chance.*

Of course, it didn't work that way. If anything, they treated me worse. I couldn't do anything right with Dave. When he saw me filling out my expense reports in my office, he sent me a nasty memo saying that I shouldn't do my expenses in the office; I should do them at home. Never mind that he did his expenses in his office, and his assistant did the same. I didn't even have an assistant—or more accurately, I had to share one with Mark Eichner, which meant in practice that I had to do everything myself. I had more work at the time than I could handle, and I could have used the help, but I didn't want to make waves, so I answered my own phone, typed my own memos, and did my own expenses. When I complained to Joe that Mark wasn't sharing his assistant with me, Joe said, "What do you want me to do? He's Mickey Eichner's son."

I'll never forget the A&R meeting when Joe set up a projector with the latest statement for one of Mark's acts. The company was losing sixteen dollars per CD on the act, but Mark smiled the whole time, as though Joe were congratulating him on a job well done.

After my promotion, Dave passed on every act I brought to him. He didn't invite me to meetings, and he slowly stripped me of any meaningful work. I felt like I had committed a capital offense, and Dave's method of execution was to ignore me to death. Even when he did invite me to an A&R conference in New York, he asked me to set up the name tags on the tables, as if I were part of the conference-hall crew, not one of his high-level employees. He was a bully, drunk with power, and I was his favorite target.

If he were a successful bully, I would have understood why Joe liked him so much. As it was, however, Dave did nothing to fix the embarrassments highlighted in the *Spy* article. For instance, we tried to sign Haddaway's "What Is Love," but we lost out to Clive Davis at Arista. That's how it went with nearly every big act we approached. We couldn't compete with Atlantic, or Sony, or any of the other majors. We relied on catalog artists like Elvis and the Pointer Sisters to hit our numbers.

In February 1993, I went to the BMG Grammy party in L.A. As the night dwindled, I found myself alone in a corner with Randy. I told him I wanted out of my marriage. He offered to help in any way he could, but he seemed startled by my admission. In a serious tone, he said he had something important to tell me. He repeated that line a few times, but before he could say whatever was on his mind, Joe appeared from out of nowhere and took him away from me. The next day, on the flight home to New York, Randy didn't mention it again, and neither did I. I thought I knew what he was going to say, and for the first time since I started at RCA, I realized how selfish and unfair I was to him. I depended on him, and I had no right to. I felt guilt and remorse.

By the spring, I knew I needed to escape from RCA. In the back of my mind, I had always hoped to return to Atlantic. With Craig Kallman rising through the ranks there, I thought he might be able to talk to Doug and help me make my way back to the only place I ever felt I belonged. I bothered Craig about it, but he said, "Doug won't have it." I felt angry at first. I did so much for Craig, but he didn't step up for me. I know now that my anger wasn't fair to him. Craig had yet to form any real power at Atlantic, so he couldn't overrule Doug Morris. But at the time, I couldn't accept it. I felt that Atlantic was my home. I couldn't deal with the prospect of never coming back. I had helped so many men succeed, but when it came time for me to get what I wanted, and what I felt they owed me, they disappeared.

Craig eventually asked me to back off, and I did. We drifted apart. When he and Isabel got married, I wasn't invited to the wedding. That hurt. To me it signaled that my old friends at Atlantic found me too controversial even for a social gathering. It also signaled that Craig— the man I spent so much time with, the man I mentored and guided, the man I once considered my closest friend—didn't want me around anymore. I took everything personally and began bad-mouthing Craig, especially after he became cochairman of Atlantic Records, a position he still holds today. He beat out Jason for that job, and it changed the course of the label, but my role was never acknowledged.

I was stuck at RCA working for a toxic boss and always on the verge of being fired. I began spinning out of control, acting in ways that were self-defeating. One morning, as I prepared to leave for work, one of Joey's mobster friends, Frankie Spodaro, showed up at our apartment.

Frankie was a member of the goon squad. Every illicit organization has a goon squad. Being born Italian in Brooklyn, I was introduced to these characters early. I was fourteen years old, home alone after school, when I saw a man in my backyard holding a metal garbage can over his head, about to throw it through the kitchen window. I ran to the phone and called my father, who ordered me to run out to the street and wait for help. I stood in the street waiting for the police, but my dad didn't call the police—he called the goon squad. Around the corner from my house was a private sanitation company (back then, all private carting companies were owned by the Mob). I looked to the corner and saw five goons running toward my house. One goon stopped to ask if I was hurt as the others dashed through the alley and into my backyard. They carried the intruder into the street and beat him up in front of me. One guy used a baseball bat.

I invited Frankie in and handed him an orange juice.

"How are you?" Frankie asked, drinking his juice.

"Unhappy," I replied. "And running late for work."

Frankie escorted me to work. As we strolled down Broadway, he quizzed me about what was bothering me. I complained about Dave Novik—how he was ruining my life, how I was afraid he was going to fire me, how I had no money and felt distraught, worried, and paranoid all the time. Frankie cut me off. "I can't take it anymore!" he yelled. "Do you have this guy's phone number?"

I told him it was in the notebook in my purse and watched, half in shock, half in amusement, as Frankie took my purse into a phone booth, dialed Dave's number, and shouted into the phone, "Dave, I'm waiting downstairs for you. I'm gonna skull-fuck you with a tire iron!"

Frankie slammed the phone down and joined me back on the street. I kissed him full on the lips.

When Dave arrived for work that day, he looked paler than usual. He told Joe that he had received a threatening phone call, and Joe called BMG security. He acted like this was a threat on the president. Of course I shouldn't have taken part in pranks like this, but it felt good. For once, Dave was having his head fucked with, and that meant he didn't have time to fuck with mine.

That afternoon, Frankie called and asked me how things were going. I said, "Can you believe Joe called BMG security?" Frankie just laughed. I didn't learn the end of the story until much later. Apparently, Frankie called Dave again that night and said, "Security ain't gonna help you."

The goon-squad incident was just a distraction, though. What really bothered me was how out of control I felt with Randy. As spring turned to summer, we went to an outdoor business lunch, and I sat across from him. It was a warm day; I wore a skirt with no pantyhose. While Randy was speaking, I inched my foot up the inside of his leg. When my foot reached his knee, he grabbed it and pushed it gently away, rubbing it the whole time, not missing a beat in his speech. He gave me a look that said, *Bad girl.* I was confused. Randy still flirted with me, but at the same time, I knew something had to change.

The more I lived by Ahmet's rules, the more isolated I became. One of my only friends left at RCA was Kenny Ortiz, the VP of R&B, and since I had increasingly little work of my own, I began helping him with frivolous tasks. For example, Kenny represented the Wu-Tang Clan, a new hit act on Loud/RCA Records. Keep in mind that the music business still didn't know what to do with hip-hop. As an art form, it had an aura of danger and was struggling to break into the mainstream. Wu-Tang had just released a single called "Wu-Tang Clan Ain't Nuthing Ta Fuck Wit," and I think they scared Kenny. They'd storm into the office demanding money, and when he'd try to explain how the payments worked—that purchase orders had to be filled out, and then he had to wait for the proper signatures before a check could be cut—they'd say, "Fuck that shit."

Since his office was near mine, I came up with a plan. I asked the security guard in the lobby to contact me when the Wu-Tang Clan came into the building. That way I could run to Kenny's office and yell, "Wu-Tang's on their way up." Kenny would then jump up from his desk, run out of his office, and dash down the stairs on the opposite side of the elevator. They'd get pissed when they couldn't find him.

Kenny also represented Martha Wash. She was most famous for her role in the group Two Tons O' Fun and the hit disco song "It's Raining Men." Martha was as lovely as she was heavy. One day Kenny left a meeting with her and came to me complaining that she hated all of his ideas and refused to sing the songs he had chosen. I asked the obvious question: "Did you offer her anything to eat?" He hadn't. Before his next meeting with Martha, I ordered a deli platter from Burke & Burke caterers, complete with a cheesecake. She was so happy at that meeting that she agreed with Kenny about everything.

Helping Kenny was a fun distraction, but it was just that: a distraction. I felt frustrated and purposeless at RCA, but I was also terrified of getting fired. Somehow Joey and I always struggled with money, even though he made six figures. I knew I couldn't count on him if I got fired—I couldn't really count on him for anything—and I didn't want to be out on my ass again.

Joey raised the stakes in the summer of 1993, when he decided to quit his job at Atlantic. He announced this decision rather than discussing it. When I asked him why he wanted to quit he said it was because Craig Kallman had dropped Marc Anthony, one of Joey's dance acts. We were both close with Marc and recognized him as a great talent (we were right: he has sold twelve million albums to date and won two Grammy Awards), but when you work at a record company, acts get dropped. That's life. Quitting over such a routine occurrence was a horrible decision. It became yet another topic for us to fight about. I had contemplated divorce before, but with my Catholic guilt and stubborn pride, it never seemed like a real possibility. Now, it seemed like the only possibility.

To make matters worse, Joey had taken an obvious interest in a redhead who lived in our building, and after he made the unilateral decision to quit his job, he had the balls to ask me to dye my hair red. I spent the summer in a full-blown depression. Every night, I went to bed next to my enemy (if he came home). Every morning I woke up with an imaginary pistol to my head. Every day, I went to a job that made me feel worthless. It was a lonely life.

By the fall of 1993, Joe and Dave had set up the gallows and were ready to walk me to it. Even my Knight in Shining Armor couldn't save me this time. Ron Fair, the senior VP of A&R on the West Coast, had signed a new act named Niki Haris. I had known Niki for a while—she sang on one of Joey's projects at Atlantic, and I spent many fun nights partying with her. Niki was now singing backup with Madonna, who was on her "Girlie Show" tour and had a run of concerts at Madison Square Garden. Joe and Dave invited me to the first show, on Thursday, October 14. It sounded like a great night. I loved Madonna and was excited to see Niki. During the week leading up to the show, Joe acted all lovey-dovey. This made me suspicious. It wasn't like him to invite me to a concert or be nice to me at work. I didn't know it at the time, but Joe was a romantic. Before he fucked a girl, he liked to take her out and set the mood.

Thursday night rolled around and I joined Joe, Dave, and Randy Goodman at MSG. Joe was his usual uptight self, and I just ignored Dave. Hanging around the two of them was a small price to pay for an evening out with Randy Goodman. The show was great, and so was Niki. We went backstage to see her after it was over, and then I went home. The next morning, I showed up for work and didn't see Joe or Randy making their normal rounds. Even Dave hadn't come in yet. This was unheard of. *I'm getting fired today*, I thought.

When Dave arrived, he asked to see me. I entered his office and could tell by his body language that he felt uncomfortable. I had no problem watching him squirm. His opening line was: "I've had an epiphany."

Oh really, I thought, as I looked at the godless man before me.

He launched into a vague lecture, drawing out every word—he needed the A&R Department to run the way he wanted it to, he had a certain way of doing things, he wanted the department to succeed, et cetera, et cetera. After fifteen minutes of listening to Dave ramble, I decided to do his job for him.

"Are you firing me?" I said.

"Yes."

"I'm outta here."

Dave was still talking as I walked out of his office. Joe was nowhere to be found. He let Dave do his dirty work, the same way that Doug had let Ahmet fire me at Atlantic. None of these men had the balls to make the final confrontation.

I went to my office, packed some stuff, asked the secretary to send the rest, and left. As I walked home, I thought of Ric Aliberte, who rarely showed up and spent $2,500 of company money on a boob job for a secretary, and Mark Eichner, who arrived at ten thirty every morning to read the paper until noon and didn't seem to understand a profit and loss statement. They still had jobs; I would have been broke if not for Randy Goodman and a $25,000 severance payment that would help bridge the gap until I could find a new job.

Do I even want a new job? I asked myself. This was a fucked-up business. I had no reason to expect that any other label would treat me better. In fact, each job seemed to treat me worse. Joe was the cruelest boss by far, making me watch a Madonna concert with him, knowing the whole time I was going to be fired the next day. It was humiliating, like he was fattening me up for the slaughter. I still can't listen to a Madonna record—it reminds me of Joe. When I told other executives in the business the story, they were shocked. It was sadistic even by their standards.

I came home to nothing—no marriage, no friends, no job. Losing RCA wasn't as painful as losing Atlantic, but it was a bigger moment of personal growth. I realized that I didn't know how to be alone. I couldn't survive without some man in the music business telling me what to do and how to feel. My influences were only men, with male perspectives. I had always known that men and women lived in different worlds, but now I relearned that lesson in a much more painful and personal way, through repeated devastation and humiliation.

As the pain subsided, I began to reflect on Randy and what he had done for me. Call it the silver lining of getting fired. I now had the space to see our relationship in its true light. In fact, that was just the word for it: light. I realized, beneath the sexual tension, what really attracted me to Randy was the light I saw in him. I couldn't articulate it, but I felt it. The light was warm and loving. The light didn't use people as tools for sex, or money, or power, the way I had been taught to do. Somewhere along the way, I had lost that light. Out of all the losses in my life, that one hurt the most. I felt thankful to Randy for showing me that the light still existed, not only in others, but also in me.

I also felt thankful for the many ways that Randy bucked the status quo and refused to take part in bystander abuse. He had little to gain by helping me secure a contract or teaching me to be a better executive. I was his subordinate, in both title and salary, and I was a woman. He could have remained a silent observer while the world of toxic masculinity did its work on me. Instead, he stepped in and tried to make a difference.

Years later, I heard through a friend that when Randy was president of Disney's Lyric Street Records and Disney decided to close the label, Randy made it his personal mission to find each of his employees a new job. My friend said, "Can you believe it?" I could. That was Randy all over. I never gave a man less and got more in return than I did with Randy Goodman.

As for Joe, I really did like him as a person when we began our journey, and I was sorry I had disappointed him. But he had disappointed me too. I went back to church on Sunday to pray, as I had done since childhood, *Forgive us our trespasses as we forgive those who trespass against us.* As a Catholic, I was taught to forgive; as an Italian, I was taught to never forget. Italians settle things in our own way, among ourselves. We reason with each other, but sometimes we have to take (or give) a beating to settle things. I knew already that I could take a beating—that's an important thing to know. I hadn't given many, though. When an opportunity presented itself to even the score with Joe, I made sure he never saw me coming.

PART III

RELATIVITY/ COLUMBIA

29

THE WAKE UP

TIM COLLINS CAME TO TOWN after the New Year. It was almost four years to the day since he let me spend the night in his hotel room after Joey threw an ashtray at my back. Tim and I had remained in contact since then. He knew what I had been through. When we met for coffee in New York, the first thing he said was, "You don't look good."

"I can't take it anymore," I said.

He drank his coffee and let me vent for a while. Then he stopped me.

"You have the same complaints every time I see you," he said, "but you're not doing anything about it. You're the only one who can change your circumstances."

"I'm worn out," I said. "Everything I do is wrong."

"When I started with Aerosmith, David Geffen suggested that I see a therapist, and it changed my life," Tim said. "You should go. It will change your life—if you want to change your life."

"I do."

Tim gave me the name of a female therapist, and he offered to pay for my sessions. This was a tremendously generous gesture—Tim has lived a life of service to others, helping many people in and out of the music business get treatment for a variety of addictions. I had health insurance, though, and I never liked taking money from anyone, even in my most broke days. I would rather eat less, buy less, and go out less than owe someone money. I thanked him and declined his offer. I did, however, take his advice. It was one of the best decisions of my life.

Therapy felt like an out-of-body experience. I could view myself objectively for the first time. I began to think about my life differently, about men differently. I told the shrink everything—the harassment, the name-calling, the arm fracturing, the mind games, the manipulation, the firings. We discussed the men in the music business, my career, and my fear of being alone. We rarely discussed Joey, strangely enough. I had checked out of the marriage so long ago that he was barely part of the problem. The therapist even said I was already past my marriage.

She began labeling these men as narcissists, addicts, and codependents; she named their behavior as passive aggression, actual aggression, and emotional manipulation. She helped me understand that my behavior was self-destructive, enabling a pattern of abuse that wouldn't stop until I stopped it. She said, "Make your own life. Don't waste time with these guys and their shit." Something about hearing it out loud brought the message home.

Through therapy, I became free in my own head. I was also free financially, at least until the money from RCA ran out. I still had a year left on my contract, and they had to pay out the remainder, which I took as a lump sum. My final check—$25,000—gave me breathing room (i.e., enough money) to reflect on the direction of my life and to plot my next move. For the first time in my career, I didn't have to rush desperately into a new job. I could decide what was best for me.

I didn't know if I wanted to work in music anymore. I knew what the men in the business thought of me—in the combined words of Irving Azoff and Dave Novik, I was an "unrelenting cunt." There are, by the way, several translations for words like "unrelenting" and "cunt" when they are used to describe a man: words such as "powerful," "decisive," and "driven." In fact, there is no shortage of positive words that people like Novik and Irving might have used to describe me if I were a man. As it stood, I seriously considered a career change. *Maybe I should go to grad school*, I thought.

While I mulled over my options, the free time hung heavy on my hands. It was winter again in New York, so I decided to make my favorite escape: I called Charlie Minor and asked if I could visit him in Los Angeles. He offered me a room in his spacious house in Beverly Hills and said he'd set up meetings for me while I visited. Charlie even had an extra car I could use. When I told Joey I was going away, he said it was improper for me to stay at Charlie's house. I don't know what pissed me off more: the hypocrisy or the jealousy. I didn't have the energy for another fight, so I booked a room at the Four Seasons Hotel.

Charlie and I had a few fun days together. We went to see Aerosmith. We had dinner with friends. Charlie arranged for me to meet with Phil Q (Quartararo), the CEO of Virgin Records. I already knew Phil from my days at Atlantic Records. He was a dwarf, but he used humor to turn his lack of height into an advantage. I often saw him at events with Ahmet, and he'd say, "I want to go up on you." In his office in L.A., he put the chairs on ground level, making him taller than anyone who sat down. I collapsed into one of these chairs and asked him what the hell I was supposed to do with my legs—I was wearing a dress. He laughed at me. We had a nice time chatting about the old days, but I had no interest in Virgin Records. I wasn't ready to return to music.

In early 1994, I visited a friend at Columbia Records. It was just a social call, or at least I intended it to be, until my friend said, "You have to meet this guy, Bob Buziak. He hates Joe Galante." Bob Buziak had been president of RCA, and Joe had worked for him before taking over the position. Now Bob was president of Relativity Records, distributed through Sony. I went up to the corporate floor where Bob had an office. When the elevator door opened, I saw a tall, elegant man in a perfectly tailored suit. It almost seemed like he was expecting me. "I'm Bob," he said, extending a hand. "I want you to tell me how badly Joe Galante treated you." He put his arm around me, led me to his office, placed a box of tissues in front of me, and asked his secretary to get me a cup of tea. "Now tell me the entire story from start to finish," he said.

As I told him about Joe's nastiness, Ric's incompetence, and Dave's coldness, he shook his head.

"I bet Joe paid them tens of thousands of dollars more than you," he said.

"Yes, yes he did," I said.

"I bet you did all the work," he said.

"Yes, yes I did."

My answers sounded like I was testifying in a Southern Baptist church.

Bob asked how I got fired, and I told him about the Madonna concert. Knowing Joe as he did, he was more disgusted than surprised by the story. After I finished my story, Bob said, "You know, Joe's done here. He failed. He's running back to Nashville."

I was shocked. There was nothing in the trades about it. As I'd later learn, when it became clear Joe was going to be fired from RCA, Joel Katz called Michael Dornemann in Germany. Joel suggested that Dornemann replace Joe in New York and allow him to return down south, keeping his New York salary while working to return RCA Nashville to its former glory. Dornemann agreed. It's nice to have Joel Katz in your corner.

"Joe's bread in Nashville, but a crumb up here," I said. Bob laughed and handed me a paper. It was a real estate listing for Joe's home in Connecticut.

"Can I have this?" I asked.

"Why?" Bob said.

"I want to send it to the press."

Bob paused for a moment. He knew that if I sent this listing to the press it would be a major embarrassment for Joe, fucking up whatever plans he had to announce his return to Nashville. He would lose control of the story, the same way he lost control of the *Spy* story. Bob said, "Do you know how to use a fax machine so it doesn't show your phone number?"

I went home with a copy of the listing and set the numbers on my fax machine to all zeros, the way Bob showed me. I faxed it to *Billboard*, *Hitmakers*, *Hits*, and *R&R* magazine, and the rumor mill started churning. Joe's grand announcement was taken out of his hands. It was payback—one Italian to another.

As the winter ended, I became bored. I had to get a job, and since the music business was all I knew, I decided to give it another shot. I called Steve Rifkind, my old pal at RCA, and asked if he had any leads.

He set up a meeting for me with Ron Urban, who also worked at RCA but had moved to Sony corporate. I couldn't thank Steve enough for his loyalty.

When I met Ron, he said that I worked hard at RCA and was an undervalued employee. This felt good—it had been so long since anyone said anything positive about my work. Ron was close with Bob Buziak, and he suggested I interview for a job at Relativity. I already liked Bob from our first meeting, so I made an appointment.

The job interview at Relativity was unique in my career. Bob didn't even want to see a résumé. He hired me on the spot as an A&R consultant for $60,000, with an expense account and travel funds, and he said I would report directly to him. I didn't have to do a song and dance; he just hired me without all the usual bullshit.

Relativity was mostly a rap label, with acts such as Bone Thugs-N-Harmony, Eazy-E (who would die the next year due to complications from AIDS), Common, and Fat Joe. The label also had some rock acts, including guitar scorchers Joe Satriani and Steve Vai. It was much smaller than the other labels I worked for—the headquarters had only just moved from Hollis, Queens, to Fifth Avenue in the city—but I loved working for Bob. He was calm, had a great sense of humor, and was the smartest man I had met in the business. Bob always treated his artists with respect. He had a natural ability to communicate with them, and he got them to do what he wanted because it was always the right move for them. He had put together a great team, hiring what I called "street executives," people who knew how to make a lot with a little. We had general manager Harry Palmer, who had previously worked for Sylvia Rhone at East West Records, marketing maven Alan Grunblatt, and Jim Cooperman from RCA in the Legal Department.

As a consultant, I didn't have to go into the office every day, but I did anyway. I liked being there. It was a place to lick my wounds and feel safe. For the first time in my career, I didn't spend every day worrying, *Is today the day I get fired?* I knew Bob was going to keep me.

I spent my time looking for bands, listening to demos, and getting back to my love of music without all the politics and egos. Bob showed me respect and treated me well. He was always around encouraging me to do what I wanted. He didn't seem to find me intimidating, overbearing, or unrelenting. He was pleasant and easy to deal with. I felt he wanted me to be part of Relativity Records. That acceptance, along with the therapy, helped me reach another step in my personal evolution.

Bob was undoubtedly my superior, but I considered him a friend. That was a first for me. Ahmet—and every other male superior I had worked for—expected deference. No matter how close we got, on some level, there was a barrier I couldn't cross. Bob was different. He'd take me out to dinner, and it felt like going out with Charlie or Frank. We'd go to the hot industry hangout—Campagna, an Italian joint—and just talk. I could say anything to him. We were open and straight with each other. There was no fear.

In the middle of 1994, Joey moved out. It shocked me, and the feeling of shock also shocked me. I knew my marriage had to end; I had known it for years. So why was Joey's exit such a jolt? Maybe it was because he was the one who acted first. It almost felt disloyal. After everything I did for him, *he* was the one to leave.

After he left, he became more successful than when he was with me. He moved into an apartment across the street, and I saw him and his new girlfriend every day. Joey and I still didn't get divorced; we stayed suspended in this state of fucked-up stasis. The therapy helped. During my year of treatment, I learned how to create boundaries and manage my caretaker personality. I no longer felt I had to fix everyone, only myself.

I finished 1994 quietly. I submitted some bands to sign, but nothing much came of them. The biggest project I worked on was an attempted buyout of Capricorn Records, a country label out of Atlanta. Capricorn had a struggling artist named Kenny Chesney, and Bob knew Kenny was going to be huge. The powers at Sony wouldn't authorize the money to buy Capricorn, though. They didn't see what Bob saw. Hell, even I understood Kenny Chesney's appeal, and I knew next to nothing about country music.

Passing on Capricorn might have seemed like the right choice—Kenny's debut album, *In My Wildest Dreams*, sold only thirty-one thousand copies, and the label went under, leaving Chesney without a record deal—but had Sony authorized the buyout, Chesney alone would have eventually paid for it ten times over. To date, he has sold thirty million records worldwide and topped the country charts twenty-nine times, and he is one of the few country artists to cross over to the pop chart, with a slew of Top 40 hits on the *Billboard* Hot 100 to his name.

Missing out on such a huge artist usually caused mortal pain to an A&R department (recall that Tunc Erim kept Bon Jovi's demo in his desk drawer at Atlantic to remind himself of that pain and make sure he never felt it again). I might have felt more devastated at losing Kenny Chesney had it happened at RCA, but I enjoyed my quiet work life at Relativity. I'd been rolling with the punches for so long that I needed a break from being punched. I took advantage of every moment to heal. I knew the break wouldn't last long.

30

HE'S GONE

MARCH 19, 1995: I WAS relaxing at home on a Sunday, getting ready to go to brunch with friends, when Bob called. His voice sounded heavy. "I just got news from the West Coast," he said. "Charlie Minor was murdered." My mind stopped working. It was a lie. It had to be a lie. As Bob told the story, I could only say one word in response: "What?" I repeated it in disbelief, over and over, *What? What? What?*

Charlie was lying in bed with his girlfriend when his ex-girlfriend, Suzette McClure, entered the house through an unlocked door, clutching a loaded gun. I knew about Suzette. She was a twenty-seven-year-old engineer who had lost her job and become a stripper and drug user. Charlie met her at a strip club, and he helped her financially while they dated. After they broke up, Suzette took a bad turn. Charlie's secretary told me Suzette had been calling constantly for the past few months and trying to track his whereabouts. Suzette also listed his Rolls-Royce for sale in the paper, a clear sign of distress that Charlie ignored. I'm sure in Charlie's mind he treated her well, but she wanted more than he could offer. Her obsession led her down a path of no return.

Suzette found Charlie in bed with his new girl and pointed the gun at them. Charlie, fast talker that he was, gentleman that he was, some-how got his girlfriend out of the room and away from Suzette. He saved his girlfriend's life. He probably thought he could handle Suzette, talk her down, and save himself. They began arguing, and she pulled the trigger several times. Charlie died from bullets to the head and body. He was forty-six years old.

Tears did not come to me immediately. The shock was too great. For a Catholic, murder stops the purpose and natural order of a life, and prayers are needed to help the victim's soul pass to the next place. In my sadness, I didn't know what else to do but pray for Charlie. As I slowly accepted the truth, my mind sputtered in the scattered, haphazard way that follows tremendous grief. My thoughts dashed first to Charlie's five-year-old daughter, Austin, who would now grow up without a father, then they zigzagged back to the mundane: Charlie was supposed to fly that evening from L.A. to Atlanta to meet Joel Katz. Don Perry was going to pick him up at the airport. I wondered what they thought of it. I forgot Joel and Don and thought of my own loss, my own sense of isolation and loneliness now that my confidant, my running partner, my sounding board, my unofficial therapist—my dear friend—was gone. I thought of Charlie's elderly mother, Jerri, and how unnatural it was to bury one's own son (I stayed in touch with Jerri until the end of her life, calling her often to check in and reminisce about Charlie). When the tears finally came, I cried for everything Charlie had meant to me, everything he had done for me, and everything he had left to do. He was an iconic force in the music business. God only knows what triumphs were in store for him.

Over the next few weeks, I heard many people in the business say terrible things about Charlie: he was a womanizer; he was asking for it; he only cared about pussy. This was heartbreaking. Yes, he had many girlfriends. Yes, he partied and lived a wild life. But if you want to know the true measure of a person, look at how he acts when the stakes are the highest. With a loaded gun in his face, Charlie had the presence of mind and the courage to make sure his girlfriend—an innocent woman—got to safety before he did. It cost him his life. That was the Charlie I knew, the Charlie I mourned. He deserved better.

I couldn't make the memorial in L.A. or the funeral in Atlanta—I didn't have the cash to travel out of state—but hundreds of people attended. It was a testament to his gift; Charlie loved people, and they loved him back. A year later, I visited his grave to pay my respects. I never got the chance to repay him for his love and kindness, but I am honored to have known him and called him a friend. I hope I see him on the other side.

31

LUCKY CRIMINALS, PART II

FOR SEVERAL YEARS, DOUG HAD been scheming to consolidate his power at Time Warner. After he had beaten out Sheldon Vogel and Jerry Greenberg as pretenders to Ahmet's throne, he pulled off a coup against Mo Ostin, the longtime chairman and CEO of Warner Bros. Records, and Lenny Waronker, the presumed heir to Ostin's throne. Doug met with Bob Morgado and pressured him to replace Ostin with a crony named Danny Goldberg. After a three-hour meeting, Morgado agreed. Ostin was ousted, Danny was hired, and Morgado issued a brief statement to the press in which he referred to Doug as "chairman and CEO" of Warner Music US, giving Doug a de facto promotion. Doug then named another crony, Val Azzoli, as president of Atlantic.

Around this time, someone in finance stumbled on numbers that didn't add up and reported it to corporate. WMG opened an investigation into its music distribution arm, including the WEA warehouse. Doug couldn't stop the investigation from happening; too many people knew about it. Instead he tried to cover his ass by ordering an investigation of his own, which found $150,000 worth of CDs missing—a comically low estimate of the money Atlantic had taken over the years. In an ill-fated attempt to make the problem go away, Doug led a few scapegoats to slaughter. One of these scapegoats was Nick Maria, longtime sales chief at Atlantic. Nick was fired on Christmas Eve without severance pay.

Meanwhile, Doug continued plotting. He had one remaining rival: Bob Morgado. In May 1995, Time Warner CEO Gerald Levin fired Morgado, reportedly because of clashes between Morgado and the heads of Warner's three principal record labels (including Atlantic). Morgado received a golden parachute—tens of millions of dollars to ease his fall— and the way was clear for Doug to become the head of WMG. But Levin didn't put Doug in charge of WMG. Instead, Levin appointed HBO chairman Michael Fuchs to the job.

After Fuchs's promotion, several negative stories about him appeared in the press. Corporate believed the stories were planted either by Doug or people in the music group under him. If Doug was involved with planting the stories, it was a fatal blunder. The chess master had just put himself in check, and checkmate wasn't long in coming.

Time Warner hired Mickey Rudin, Frank Sinatra's longtime lawyer, to conduct a separate investigation. The company also rehired Nick Maria and Richard Steinberg, who regularly traveled with Doug when he was VP of A&R at Atlantic. Rudin interviewed Nick, with Time Warner's corporate lawyer present in the room. As it turned out, Doug had picked the wrong scapegoat.

Nick explained how Atlantic used cleans, overruns, and cut-outs to profit from artists. He compiled a list of two hundred people who had asked for, or received, gifts bought with the stolen money. He listed the gifts: US Open tickets, televisions, Cartier watches, golf clubs. "The only thing I didn't buy was underwear and socks," Nick said. These gifts made up a small fraction of the money stolen, however. Most of the cash was used for hookers. Nearly every man in the company/corporation got a blow job. After the interview ended, Warner's corporate attorney turned to Nick and said, "How come you never got me a blow job?"

Rudin's investigation also found that Doug had purchased an apartment for his assistant, Joan Brooks, with company money. The apartment was in Battery Park, in the same building where Sylvia Rhone lived. This led Rudin to uncover Doug's long history of questionable relationships with women—Doug's Dolls et al.

On June 21, 1995, Fuchs called Doug to his office at HBO. Doug had no idea of Rudin's investigation, and he reportedly thought Fuchs was finally going to promote him to run Warner's Global Music Division.

Instead, Fuchs handed him a press release that read DOUG MORRIS
RELIEVED OF ALL RESPONSIBILITIES AT WARNER MUSIC GROUP. It was
a fucked-up way to fire someone—the type of thing Doug might have
appreciated if he wasn't on the receiving end. Security guards sealed
Doug's office at 75 Rock, and when he returned, they wouldn't let him
in. A "senior Warner source" was quoted as saying, "It's like there is
a God after all. It's a little like at school when the bully finally gets his
comeuppance."

While all this was happening, another of Doug's cronies, Mel Lewinter, was being fired. Guards sealed Lewinter's office and broke into safe.

That night, Doug placed a desperate phone call to Ahmet. He
wanted Ahmet to leave Atlantic and follow him in a show of solidarity.
Doug, the great reader of people, had made perhaps the most crucial
misread of his career. Ahmet had no solidarity with anyone but Ahmet.
Naturally, he refused, saying he couldn't quit his own company. Doug
called him a "fucking traitor" and hung up on him. Ahmet said they
never spoke again.

From my safe perch at Relativity, it felt good to watch Doug fall.
It was the closest to justice I'd ever get after the way he fired me from
Atlantic. Of course, justice works on a sliding scale for rich men in
corporate America.

The details get a bit complicated, but it is a perfect example of how
men like Doug used their influence and connections to ensure they'd
never pay the price for their actions, so it is worth describing in some
detail. Before Doug was fired, he signed artist-songwriter Bruce Roberts
to Atlantic. Doug and Bruce shared a lawyer, Ina Meibach, and in late
1994, Doug promoted her to executive vice president of Warner Music
US—another crony placed in power. When Doug was fired, Meibach
called Bruce and asked him to speak with Edgar Bronfman Jr. on Doug's
behalf, adding that it was "911"—meaning, an emergency. Bruce placed
the call, asking Bronfman to "call off the dogs" on Doug. Bruce and
Bronfman were best friends and songwriting partners. Bronfman was
heir to the Seagram Company fortune, as well as a large shareholder in
Time Warner. He had just purchased MCA, Polygram, and Universal
Pictures, and would soon form them into Universal Music Group, one
of the biggest labels in the world. Bronfman later gave Doug a label deal

called Rising Tide under MCA, setting the stage for Doug to take over at Universal Music Group. It was another example of how Doug used the relatives of wealthy, influential people to help his career.

Back then MCA was a joke. People called it Music Cemetery of America, because it was in last place among major labels and had little more than an impressive back catalog to boast about. But it gave Doug a chance, and that's all he needed. In November 1995, five months after being fired for cause, Doug was named chairman and CEO of what would become Universal Music Group.

It gets worse. Because Michael Fuchs had fired Doug for cause, he had no intention of paying the remainder of Doug's lucrative contract. When Fuchs himself was fired, Terry Semel and Bob Daly took over the Music Division at Time Warner. Doug counted both men as close friends. They paid out his contract.

The story has a predictable coda: five years later, Doug was one of the highest-paid executives in the music business even though UMG was among several labels involved in a price-fixing scandal (some estimates say that between 1995 and 2000, consumers were overcharged on CDs to the tune of nearly $500 million).

32

BREAK UP

IN THE MIDDLE OF MY schadenfreude over Doug's firing, I took Joey to court. I didn't have enough money to get a divorce—I couldn't afford counsel or court fees—so I had to figure it out on my own. I learned I didn't need a lawyer in family court. A social worker helped me file papers for spousal support. Joey and I didn't have assets, so it wasn't a messy process. At the hearing, I didn't ask for anything specific. The judge asked how much I wanted, and I answered, "However much you think is appropriate." I was humble—maybe too humble. I could have dragged it out, but I just wanted it to be over. The judge ordered Joey to pay for my health insurance and rent for three months, until we worked out a deal, as well as $13,500 divided into bimonthly payments. That got his attention. Despite his six-figure salary, he acted like I was taking him for everything he was worth.

Under the terms of legal separation, as long as Joey and I lived apart for more than a year, our divorce automatically became final. He had already moved out; we just had to keep it that way. Technically we were still married, and I kept his name—most people in the business knew me as Dorothy Carvello, and it was just so easy to pronounce. Joey still lived across the street from me with his new girlfriend, but I accepted our new arrangement. He tried to retaliate by threatening to sue for custody of the dogs, but I called his bluff and gave them to him. He returned them the next day.

In December 1995, I went through a more painful separation. Bob Buziak announced he was leaving Sony. He'd grown tired of the internal politics and was especially disgusted over losing the fight to sign Capricorn Records and Kenny Chesney. I understood his feelings and didn't begrudge him for leaving, but I had three months left on my contract and didn't know what Bob's departure would mean for my job at Relativity. We had no boss until March 1996 (a month after my divorce became final), when Sony appointed Sal Licata as the new president of RED Distribution, which included Relativity. I didn't know Sal, and I never got the chance. Before he started, I got a call from Jim Cooperman telling me that Sal was going to drop me and didn't want to pay the remainder of my salary. Jim was appalled but told me not to worry—Sony had a legal obligation to pay off my contract.

I felt grateful for Jim's loyalty and his assurance that I'd be paid. I also felt grateful to Bob. This was the best firing I had experienced. I didn't leave in shame or anger. No one fucked me over. In fact, I left Relativity feeling better about myself than when I came in. That was a first. The past two years had been uneventful ones for my career, but momentous ones for my personal life. I now understood that there were men in the business who would treat me with respect, and I could return that respect. I understood that there were workplaces where I could feel safe, where I didn't have to live in constant fear of being fired or harassed. I had Bob to thank for that.

None of it changed the bottom line, though. I was out on my ass again, in need of a job. I stood at another crossroads in my career. I had lost four jobs in nine years and was running out of places to go in the music business. I looked ahead to my thirty-fourth birthday (for some reason, I always needed a job around my birthday) and began thinking those familiar thoughts: *Do I want another job in music? Should I find a new career? What comes next?* I went to church and prayed for a sign.

33

PAGE SIX

Settling into my morning routine, I opened the *New York Post* and flipped to the Page Six gossip column. At the top of the page, in the plum spot, was a hatchet job on Donnie Ienner, chairman of Columbia Records. Someone inside Columbia had gone to the press and said Donnie had a big mouth, was too demanding, and was slipping from his number one perch. The mystery informant also called Donnie's brother, record producer Jimmy Ienner, a has-been.

It was mean.

I called a friend at Columbia and tried to gauge the reaction at the office. She said Donnie was furious, stomping around and demanding to know who had talked to Page Six. Donnie surely knew that everyone in the business had read the article by now, and in the vain, petty world of music executives, he knew he couldn't let such a humiliation go unanswered. Someone's head had to roll.

I couldn't imagine who would dare cross him, let alone in such a public way. This was different from the *Spy* magazine article about RCA. Joe Galante didn't inspire fear; Donnie was terrifying. Not only was he physically massive, he walked around like he had a twenty-foot dick. Sensing an opportunity to get in his good graces, I set up a meeting with Larry Jenkins, senior vice president of publicity for Columbia. When I got to Larry's office, he looked exhausted. I could see the toll Donnie's anger had taken.

"Rough day?" I said.

"You have no idea," he said.

I cut right to my pitch. "What if I could find out the source of the story for you?" I asked. "Do you think Donnie would hire me?"

"Donnie rewards loyalty," he said. "This could be huge."

As soon as I got home, I called every journalist I knew. That night I also went to Elaine's, a restaurant that was a local hangout for writers, and I chatted them up about the Page Six story. No one could tell me what I wanted to know. In fact, they were worse than useless— they pumped *me* for stories about Donnie. I said I didn't know him well, but I knew how tough and brutally honest he was. I knew from personal experience how those qualities could be misconstrued. Whatever Donnie's faults were, I told them, you couldn't argue with success. Columbia Records was the top label in the business.

I left Elaine's without anything useful, but I had other cards to play. The following night the *New York Post* held its annual Liberty Medal awards ceremony at Gracie Mansion, and I attended with the intention of meeting Richard Johnson, who was both the editor of Page Six and the author of the article in question. Entering the mansion, I spotted Richard immediately. He was tall and handsome. He looked like a movie star. I introduced myself and commented on the Page Six story. "There must be a leak at Sony," I said. He laughed. I grilled him with questions about the leak, but he told me nothing. However, based on gossip I believed to be true, I had my own suspicions that the person was a big shot within Sony. I left the ceremony with a sense of dread. If my hunch was right, the culprit was someone I didn't want to cross.

I went home and weighed my options. If I told Larry the truth about who I thought planted the story, I might never work in the music business again (that's how powerful this guy was). At the same time, if I was right and Donnie found out about it, he might offer me a job. The last time I had encountered Donnie—in Los Angeles for Grammy week, during my Atlantic days—I decided I could never work for him. But things had changed, and working for Columbia would be a huge step up from where I had been the past few years.

Larry's words rang in my head: *Donnie rewards loyalty.* I plucked up my nerve and invited Larry to my apartment. *He'll never believe me*, I thought nervously as I waited for him to show up. When Larry arrived, I found out he had a hunch of his own.

"Did the name Dr. Rock Positano come up?" he asked. Positano was dating Lisa Mottola, Tommy's ex-wife, and Tommy had asked Larry to find out if Positano was the leak. If my hunch was correct, this was a devious move meant only to fuck with Positano.

"No," I said. "I think I know who planted the story." He gave me an inquiring look, and I took a leap of faith. "Tommy Mottola."

I had just accused the boss, the capo, the don of Sony—a man who flashed guns during business meetings—of screwing over his number two man. Tommy was known for using the press to keep his executives in line. His public relations man was Dan Klores, one of the most powerful and connected PR men in the business. At the time, Donnie Ienner was trying to renegotiate his contract, and it all seemed to add up. I believed that Tommy had planted the story so that when Donnie requested more money, he could say, "Sorry, you got bad press for the company." Truly devious.

It felt like forever until Larry responded. "I totally believe that," Larry said.

My blood pressure dropped back to a normal level.

"Tommy has been acting funny," Larry continued. "He won't get off my ass, calling me all day to see if anyone has found out who leaked the story, acting like he's all upset for Donnie."

Unfortunately, Larry said, Donnie would never believe it—he thought Tommy was his best friend. Larry offered $10,000 for the information and made me swear an oath of omertà (the Mafia code of silence). He said I could pick up the money the next day from the doorman at his apartment building. He also said he would have a conversation with Donnie about my situation at Relativity. Maybe there would be a job for me at Columbia. I was skeptical, but at least I had ten grand to pay my rent.

Two weeks later, I received a call from Donnie Ienner's office, asking me to meet him for breakfast at EJ's Luncheonette on the East Side. I arrived early and ordered tea. At exactly 9:30 Donnie walked in. He looked like money, wearing a Hugo Boss suit, a Boss white shirt, and a Ferragamo tie. I had forgotten what a striking figure he was in person—tall and muscular, his perfect smile gleaming underneath a slightly crooked nose. He greeted me with a handshake and a boisterous hello. "Dorothy, it's great to see you. Thank you for defending me."

The greeting took me off guard. This wasn't the same Donnie I had met in a bungalow at the Beverly Hills Hotel. Maybe my loyalty had paid off.

"You're welcome," I said. "I know what it is like to be judged by people who don't know you."

Donnie seemed more interested in getting to know me than he did at our first meeting all those years before. Settling into the chair opposite me, he peppered me with questions. "What was it like working for Ahmet?" he asked.

"Well, I've come to realize that I was only ever meant to work at Atlantic Records," I said. "But Ahmet should come with a warning label: prolonged exposure can cause harm."

His laugh sounded like a roar. He went on to Irving, and I realized now that I was on trial: *Dorothy Carvello v. the Men of the Music Business*, the Honorable Donnie Ienner presiding.

"What happened at Giant?" he asked.

"I don't know; I got fucked. But Irving's wife . . . jeez."

"What about Craig Kallman?" he asked, moving through the men in my career. *He did his research this time*, I thought.

"Well, it worked out good for Craig," I said. "But Doug blocked me from getting back to Atlantic."

"I know you worked for Joe," Donnie said. "What's with him and Goodman?"

"They're like Frick and Frack," I said. "Joe likes to pretend he's just a hick from Nashville, but he's way more cunning and dangerous than he gets credit for."

"Why did he fire you?"

"Two words: Dave Novik. He tortured me for almost two years!"

When I said I hated Dave, Donnie said he did too. He said that he'd had nothing to do with hiring him, that it was Tommy's idea. In Donnie's opinion, Novik had no clue and no balls. Most damning of all was the time Novik heard Billy Joel's "We Didn't Start the Fire" and didn't want to release it as a single. He said it wasn't a hit (it went to the top of the *Billboard* Hot 100 and earned a Grammy nomination for Song of the Year). Finally, I felt vindicated. I always saw Dave Novik as Tommy from the Who's eponymous rock opera—deaf, dumb, and blind. Joe made me feel wrong for thinking that, but how wrong could I be if a man running an $800 million company agreed with me?

The cross-examination ended with Bob Buziak (we both agreed that Bob was a great guy and it was a shame he left Sony), and Donnie made an offer. "I'm going to pick up your contract from Relativity," he said. "You'll have an expense account and a computer, you can travel, and I'll pay for you to hire a lawyer." He certainly knew how to treat a girl. I wanted to accept the offer, but I had one reservation. I told Donnie the truth: I didn't want to work within the normal A&R Department setting. It was too damaging after what I had been through, especially with Novik. I didn't even want to be a full-time employee. I needed something different.

"No problem," Donnie said. "You can report to John Ingrassia. He's the general manager."

That was easy, I thought. In the time it took to finish breakfast, I had a new job, an expense account, the freedom to hire my own lawyer, and permission to report directly to Columbia's general manager. Donnie had clearly done his research on me, but he still gave me a chance at the top label in the business.

34

WE'RE NUMBER ONE (COLUMBIA)

COLUMBIA RECORDS WAS ENORMOUS. THE headquarters took up three floors (twenty-four, twenty-five, and twenty-six) of the Sony building at 550 Madison Avenue, and the label was home to nearly three hundred artists. I came in as an A&R consultant. My job was to find new music and bring it to the attention of John Ingrassia, Don DeVito, and Will Botwin. Columbia had a huge A&R staff, but I felt they would be more competition than help, so I kept mostly to myself. I didn't ask Donnie for a permanent place in A&R either. I knew how easily I could be fired again. I was afraid to push my luck.

I spent most days hanging out on twenty-six near the Press Department, or on twenty-five near the offices of the senior VP of promotion, Jerry Blair, and his number two man, VP of promotion Charlie Walk. I knew Charlie Walk from Kiss 108, the radio station where he used to work. He was small in stature but had the biggest personality in any room. I knew Jerry Blair too. Charlie Minor once invited me, Jerry, and about twenty other people out to dinner, and when Charlie left the table toward the end of the meal, Jerry yelled for everyone to run out of the restaurant, leaving Charlie with the massive check.

In some ways, Jerry and Charlie were stereotypical promotion men. They lived a wild lifestyle and could always be counted on for a touch of insanity. One day I got off the elevator on twenty-five to find a herd of lambs bleating and baaing all over the place. Mariah Carey was coming up to do some radio calls, and since she called her fans "lambs," the two of them put on this display for her. At the same time, Jerry and Charlie didn't do the shit that gave promotion men a bad reputation (for instance, one man masturbated on his secretary's desk in front of her). Quite the contrary, Charlie supported me from the start and sometimes let me do my work in his office. Sadly, other women apparently weren't so lucky. Charlie eventually became president of Republic Records, and as of this writing he and Republic have agreed to part ways after several women accused him of sexual misconduct.

As for Jerry, he hired many female executives, including Cynthia Johnson, Columbia's first female African American senior vice president; Elaine Locatelli, another senior VP; and Lisa Ellis, who became the president of R&B music. He was truly devoted to his female employees. When one of them wanted to start a family, Jerry allowed her to work from home on Fridays so she could spend time with her children. Several male department heads complained, but Jerry stood his ground and placated them by extending work-from-home Fridays to male executives as well.

Both men worked hard. We had a weekly scheduling meeting to set the priorities for radio promotion, and Jerry, who had over a hundred people reporting to him from all over the nation, likened it to being an air traffic controller. Each week he had records landing in different cities—Miami, L.A., Phoenix, New York—and he had to figure out how to route them so they didn't crash into other records we were trying to get off the ground.

The Promotion Department did its radio pitches on Mondays and Tuesdays. Wednesdays, all the official ads were made. Thursdays and Fridays, the trade magazines listed all the hit records from the week. Outlets such as *R&R*, *Radio and Records*, and *Billboard* let us know how we were doing.

Donnie kept a close eye on his promotion team. He came from a promotion background, running that department for Clive Davis at Arista Records. These guys couldn't bullshit him. Even I was afraid of him. Donnie didn't give you the chance to kiss his ass. You had to move at his pace. He worked like lightning—he'd return the calls, attend the meetings, and leave every night at seven with his day done. That's the mark of a great executive.

Politically correct he was not. He called male executives pussies. He made grown men making millions of dollars a year cower like babies. Donnie never turned his temper on me. I loved watching him in action. From where I stood, he represented long-overdue justice. For years I'd had to put up with the male-culture bullshit. Watching Donnie ream these guys out almost made up for all the other men at all the other labels that had fucked with me. It also gave me a measure of safety: Donnie hired me and approved of me, so that meant anyone I needed at the company had to work with me, no questions asked. If they had complaints about me, they could feel free to tell Donnie. Good luck with that!

Maybe his methods were unorthodox, but Donnie got results. On his watch, Columbia had been the top label six years in a row. He demanded excellence from those who worked for him because he demanded it from himself. He was hardworking and brilliant, with a natural ability to keep the entire business in his head, like Doug. One instance sums it all up: Donnie came in on a Saturday (he'd work weekends if he had to) and saw an employee from the R&B Division there as well. The two men left the office and walked to the garage together, where Donnie noticed that they had the same make and model Mercedes. The following Monday Donnie quietly ordered a review of the R&B Department spending. He knew the executive's salary and what his car cost, and he knew it didn't add up. The review found financial irregularities, and Donnie fired the R&B executive.

As intimidating as he could be, Donnie understood how to motivate and get the most out of his staff. This is an innate gift that can't be taught in business school. He knew that not every horse can be ridden, but every horse has a use. He understood that A&R men were like talent, and sometimes their personality quirks had to be overlooked. For instance, John Kalodner was working for Columbia on the West Coast as senior VP of A&R. He once didn't come to work for three days and said he was boycotting the office. Donnie called him to ask why, and Kalodner said he wanted the dividers of the men's room urinals to have more privacy (that's exactly the sort of thing Kalodner would do).

Donnie had the urinals reconstructed to Kalodner's liking. Of course, this was also an example of how men get special treatment, but Donnie knew Kalodner's value and knew he had to keep him happy.

His decision-making skills went beyond the music business, too. One of the secretaries at Columbia was dating a promotion executive in the company, and after they split up, he refused to return a rug of hers. She went to see Donnie about it. Donnie said he was happy she broke up with her boyfriend and then called the guy in front of her. "Return her stuff or I'll fucking fire you, fatso," Donnie said. You can't argue with success.

I had only one run-in with Donnie. During my first year at Columbia, I tried to sign the band Creed. They were making some noise locally in Tallahassee, Florida, and my lawyer, Nick Ferrara, brought them to my attention. I knew they would be a hit: the lead singer, Scott Stapp, sounded just like Eddie Vedder of Pearl Jam. At that time, Pearl Jam was in the middle of a vicious fight with Ticketmaster over concert ticket prices, and the band suffered commercially. This left a huge void in rock radio, and I thought Creed could fill it.

I submitted Creed's demo to Botwin, DeVito, and Ingrassia, with a note that the deal would only cost us $50,000, which I knew was a steal for a band with so much potential. Botwin passed because he said it sounded like Eddie Vedder. *That's the fucking point*, I thought. All I could do was watch as Creed went to another label and released *My Own Prison*, which went six times platinum on the backs of four number one singles. The band's next release, 1999's *Human Clay*, is one of ninety albums in history to earn a diamond certification (ten million sales). Yet again, my ear was vindicated. Yet again, it didn't matter.

After Creed became a hit, Jerry Blair came to see me. He'd just been in a meeting with Donnie, Botwin, and DeVito. At the meeting, Donnie was complaining and reaming the promotion guys out for not having more hits. Jerry said, "Why don't you sign what Dorothy brings in, like Creed?" Donnie never even knew I had submitted Creed. The A&R department didn't pass along my suggestions to him. When Jerry told me this, I went home angry and faxed Donnie the original memo I had written on the band, as well as Botwin's pass notes. I never heard back.

The bullshit with Creed made me lose a little more of my confidence. Just like when I was a child, it seemed every time I tried to stick my head up above the pack, someone smacked it down. I had come to Columbia already feeling that I couldn't trust my ears. Now I felt that even when my ears were right, no one would listen to me anyway. Creed was just the latest in a series of breaks that could have made my career—breaks that I missed not because someone else worked harder or performed better, but because I was ignored.

I decided the best defense was to lie low at Columbia. I didn't want any more trouble. So what if they passed on my bands? *Keep your head down and collect your salary*—that was my motto. And yet, I couldn't help but admit that there was something sick about the business, something that had scarred me, something that, as I would soon find out, could infect even the purest heart.

35

HE'S GONE TOO

NOVEMBER 22, 1997: AHMET CALLED in the middle of the night. "What are you doing?" he said. I was living alone, enjoying a quiet life and a quiet mind, and I didn't appreciate the intrusion. It reminded me of when I worked for him and he'd call at all hours expecting me to find him a hooker.

"I'm sleeping, Ahmet, what do you think I'm doing?" I said.

"You are not going to believe this," he said. From his voice, I could tell something was wrong.

"Just tell me."

"Michael Hutchence committed suicide."

I tried to process Ahmet's words, but they hung there, refusing to make sense. Just like when I heard about Charlie, I could only say one word: "What?"

"Come see me as soon as you can," Ahmet said and hung up.

The next day, I got dressed without thinking and hopped into a cab. After what felt like eternity crawling from my apartment on the West Side to Ahmet's townhouse on the East Side, one of his servants squired me into the living room, where Ahmet was pacing frantically. He immediately began questioning me: When did I last see or speak to Michael? Did it seem like he was in trouble? The questions distracted us for a few moments from the darkness we wished to avoid.

Ahmet offered me a drink. I took a glass of wine to dull the pain. He continued pacing, lighting one cigarette after another. He took the loss as hard as anyone—for all his faults, he truly loved his artists. I realized that by calling me and inviting me to be with him, Ahmet was also showing me love.

"He was too young," I said. I put my face in my hands and cried. I had experienced death before, but never with someone so close to my age. Ahmet got up and placed his hand on my shoulder. Normally I cringed at Ahmet's touch, but this time he wasn't groping. He was consoling. I welcomed the solace. I needed it.

"I don't understand," I said to Ahmet, stifling a sob. "If Michael could kill himself, what chance do the rest of us have?"

Ahmet explained that because of the nature of creativity, artists were more prone to dark thoughts and moods. It was worse if they were drinking and taking drugs. His words were surprisingly calming. He had clearly seen this sort of thing before—Ahmet was close to R&B singer Donny Hathaway, who committed suicide under suspicious circumstances in 1979.

Thinking of all the people in music who had either committed suicide or died under fucked-up circumstances, I couldn't help but wonder if there was something more to Michael's death. He was nearing his fortieth birthday and INXS wasn't as big as they once were. Maybe he didn't want to trot out onstage to play the old hits anymore. Maybe he feared losing relevance. That's how the game works—one minute you're riding the top of the wave, the next minute you're sucked under the water. *Maybe this is just what the music business does to people*, I thought.

My only consolation was that Michael was Protestant, which meant he could have a funeral. The Catholic Church doesn't allow funerals for victims of suicide, punishing you even in death for taking your own life. It was small comfort, though. Michael was still gone.

Ahmet asked me to grab a pad and a pen and take dictation as he prepared a statement for the press. We had come full circle—Ahmet, the larger-than-life boss; and me, the secretary who still couldn't take dictation. Ahmet spoke about Michael's brilliant songwriting and his thrilling live performances. He said Michael's music would live on, and he would forever be a part of the Atlantic family. Then, perhaps for my benefit, he added, "My secretary said he had a big dick." I put my pen down and looked at him, laughing and crying at the same time, wondering how that was even possible. "I never said that," I told Ahmet. "But now that you brought it up . . ." We both laughed.

Ahmet was truly wonderful that day. He helped me make sense of my devastation. He told me that we had to go on, to keep living, because moving forward was the only cure for heartbreak. I wasn't used to the insightful, tender, and loving Ahmet, but I liked him. I wished he showed this side of himself more often. He was an enigma to me always.

Over the next few weeks, the news was full of stories about Michael and his legacy. The best tribute, though, came from the radio stations that played his songs, reminding anyone who cared to listen of the beauty Michael brought into the world.

When an artist dies, fans often feel like they've lost a close friend. In my case, however, I was both a fan and a close friend. My mind flashed back to ten years earlier on the second floor of Atlantic Records, when he came alive out of MTV and into my office with the biggest smile I'd ever seen and even bigger brown eyes.

I remembered his charisma, his passion, and his wicked sense of humor. He did excellent impressions—he'd imitate Ahmet and Mick Jagger having a conversation until tears of laughter streamed down my face. Or he'd make me play the secretary (a role that didn't require much acting) while, in a spot-on version of Ahmet's frog croak, he'd say, "Ahh, ahh, get me a hooker and some hash." Out of every man I knew in the music business, he was the only one who could crack me up like that.

Now, that beautiful baritone voice was silenced. All I had left were memories. All I could do was move forward, like Ahmet told me to do, and hope that I'd see Michael again. I was racking up too many appointments on the other side.

36

TOP BANANA

IN FEBRUARY 1998, I RECEIVED an invitation to Clive Davis's annual Grammy Eve party at the Beverly Hills Hotel, and I went with my friend, gossip columnist Roger Friedman. At the party, Roger and I were seated at the same table as Ahmet and his two dates. Ahmet saved me a seat next to him and introduced me to the table as the best secretary he ever had. He started laying on the bullshit—talking about the bands I signed for him, calling me a "truly talented woman." I cut in: "Ahmet's too kind. I couldn't type or take dictation." Everyone laughed.

As the festivities got under way, Ahmet complimented me on my appearance and told me how much he missed me. Then, with a straight face, he said, "Now that we aren't working together anymore, it would be okay for us to date." I don't know why this comment surprised me, but it did. There was so much wrong with it, including Ahmet's sudden respect for the rules of the Human Resources Department. If Ahmet wanted to date his secretary, or any other coworker, nothing would stop him. I knew that. He knew that.

"Ahmet," I replied, "you already fucked me with that twenty-five-dollar Christmas bonus you gave me, and the shitty bonus Doug gave me for signing Skid Row." He laughed and said he'd give me all the money I wanted, that our relationship transcended money. Before I could come up with a witty reply, he shoved his hand between my legs and began tugging at my panties. I slapped his hand, smiling the whole time, trying to avoid a scene, hissing through my teeth, "Get the fuck off me or I'm going to throw water in your face." I couldn't make him stop; even at nearly seventy-five years old, he was still incredibly strong. Soon we were hitting each other in full view of the dinner guests.

I finally freed myself from Ahmet's grasp and made Roger switch seats with me. At the end of the dinner, Ahmet leaned over the table and gave me his room number at the Peninsula, saying, "After this, meet me at the hotel and we can listen to some music." Ahmet really was unbelievable. The last time I'd seen him, he'd helped me make sense of Michael's tragic death. This time, he was back to being Classic Ahmet— back to groping, harassing, taking advantage of his position and power. For reasons too numerous to mention, I decided not to take Ahmet up on his offer. He remained my mentor and friend, but our relationship remained as complicated as ever.

In September, I received a call from Ahmet's office saying that Noreen Woods, Ahmet's longtime assistant, had died. I was invited to the wake and went to pay my respects. It was a beautiful ceremony. Ahmet enlisted the cabaret singer and pianist Bobby Short to play the piano and sing "I'll Be Seeing You." Ahmet also gave a moving eulogy. It showed that he had the capacity to act like a normal, decent human being. He could give a lovely, heartfelt tribute to a woman who had devoted so much of her life to him. But Classic Ahmet always stood in the wings, waiting to rear his ugly head.

After the service, Ahmet hosted an event at a restaurant a block over. When I arrived, I saw him sitting at a large table surrounded by his Chiquitas—I called them Chiquitas because they were usually blonde and came in bunches just like bananas. He saw me and motioned me over. "Sit next to me," he said, ushering one of the Chiquitas out of the way so I could take her place. As I sat down, I noticed that the Chiquita on the other side of Ahmet looked familiar. Ahmet said to her, "I want you to meet my secretary, Dorothy." I shook hands with the woman. *Where do I know her from?* Then it hit me—it was Charlie Minor's ex, the woman who was in bed with him just before he was killed. She had become part of Ahmet's posse.

So there I was, the main Chiquita, seated next to the king, part court jester and part loyal subject. I didn't have long to reflect on the moment before I felt an all-too-familiar sensation: Ahmet shoving his hand between my legs. He tugged at my panties.

"What the fuck is wrong with you?" I said. "We're at a memorial. Why don't you stop for five seconds?"

"Have a drink," he said. "Loosen up."

"I'm loose."

I tried to hit him away, but force had never worked before and it didn't work now. If Ahmet wanted to grab a pussy, he was strong enough to do it no matter the objections. Trying to divert his attention, I said, "By the way, where's Doug?" I had noticed that Doug, in a predictably classless move, didn't come to Noreen's funeral even though Noreen's sister Joan was like his second mother. He let his feud with Ahmet come first. Doug had no excuse. I came although I didn't feel comfortable at Atlantic events. Even Sylvia Rhone came—I saw her crying in the restaurant. My question stopped Ahmet's groping. "I don't know," Ahmet said. "I guess he didn't come."

Something about that moment brought my life into fresh focus. A decade before, I revered these men and based my life and career on them. Ten years later, I was sitting in a restaurant surrounded by Ahmet's girlfriends, batting away yet another of Ahmet's drunken attempts to paw at my body, noticing that Doug didn't even have the courage to show up. It all seemed so *sad*.

Ahmet, I realized, was aging disgracefully. There was no reflection, no lessons learned. He still snorted cocaine and drank to excess. Maybe he needed a Viagra every now and then to spark his fire, but he'd still take a girl into the Atlantic bathroom in the middle of the day and grope his Chiquitas all night. He had a harder time partying because of a recent hip replacement and a fractured pelvis, but it seemed that nothing short of death could stop him. For the first time, I understood that the freedom that always attracted me to Ahmet was also a prison.

37

SHE'S GONE

THE SUMMER OF 1999 WAS the longest of my life. My mother began complaining of stomach pains, and her doctor said she had an ulcer. Over the coming weeks, she deteriorated to the point where she couldn't walk. I took her to a new doctor, who immediately admitted her to the hospital with a new diagnosis: colon cancer.

It never occurred to me that her cancer would return. I didn't want to believe it. "If I could trade places with you, I would," I told her as she went into the hospital. Surgery proved ineffective—the cancer was too far advanced—and the doctor said she had a matter of months to live. She was only sixty-five years old.

There was nothing to do but take her home and try to make her comfortable. She decided to kick my father out after nearly half a century of living together. I saw it as her last attempt to control her life. I took my three dogs and moved in with her. I tried to keep working but spent nearly every second providing care. I lost twenty pounds. My life changed overnight as I tried to help my mother through this nightmare.

Watching my mother suffer, I learned that the human body has a process while it dies. Each day brings another frightening change. The mind also begins a process of introspection. She spoke about her regrets and disappointments, and it took every ounce of strength I had not to cry or crack up. She said she didn't want to die, that she wanted more time, and her words stuck in me like knives. She was my first role model, and now I saw how a life lived by her example would end. I always felt my mother got a bum deal in life. Her family beat her down. She was the perpetual problem solver, but no one helped her with her problems. She never had nice things, never got a vacation, never experienced the tender side of life, and now she'd never get the chance.

As summer passed into fall, and fall into winter, she dwindled closer and closer to death. One weekend in December, she began to slip in and out of consciousness, and her doctor came to the house to tell her it was time to go into hospice. There was no in-home hospice back then, and she left the house reluctantly. We all went to see her at the hospice center that day, and my brother spent a restless night with her. The priest came the next day and gave her the last rites. I asked my mother if she wanted me to call my father and she laughed. She said not having him around was the best three months of her life.

My mother talked about her dead relatives and said she saw them in the room with her. She saw her father and her sister Carole, who died when I was six years old. Then she began to draw heavy, labored breaths. She squeezed my hand. I was frightened, but her face was peaceful. I saw a white light around her as she breathed her last. The priest was there with us and said she was at peace. The doctors and nurses said she had a good death; she only spent one day in hospice. She kept her dignity and was impeccably put together until the end—hair, makeup, and nails. It's funny how these small details are often all we have left in the face of death.

My mother died on December 23, and since the Catholic Church doesn't bury on Christmas, she had to stay in the morgue until the holiday passed. I went back to Brooklyn with my brother and sister, while my older brother went to the pork store to buy us all something to eat. He bought me a ham sandwich with roasted peppers. It seemed like months since I had eaten and just as long since I had enjoyed it.

My father came to meet us, and as soon as he entered, I began yelling at him. I blamed him for my mother's death. He just took all the shit I heaped on him and began to cook for the crowd that had gathered. I went home alone and cried the entire night. It felt so fucking unfair. I tried to live an honorable life. I went to church every Sunday. Why didn't God answer my prayers, my novenas? Why did my mother have to suffer?

On Christmas Eve I went to the funeral home and made arrangements to get my mother's body out of the hospice morgue. Then I went to my parents' house to get an outfit and her rosary beads in preparation for the funeral. When I entered, I saw a Hallmark scene—my cousins, siblings, and family friends were eating Christmas Eve dinner. I was stunned. *How can Christmas go on when I am suffering in grief?* Nothing seemed to make sense.

On Christmas Day I went to the funeral home with the clothes and the rosary and they prepared my mother's body for the funeral. The next day, we held a wake. It was a surreal event. My mother thought no one loved her or appreciated her, but the number of people there proved how many lives she had touched. Everyone had a story of her compassion and kindness. Of course, in the midst of this heartwarming scene came the normal family bickering. Italians have a rule: weddings and funerals are the time and place to air all one's grievances with other family members. I was prepared; I rented two rooms in the funeral home, one for the viewing and a private lounge for fights.

I had not yet cried. I was too overwhelmed. Death is more than just devastation. There are so many practical concerns that must be handled, and because of my role in the family, I had to handle them all; that left me no time to process what had happened. Then, in the funeral home, I felt a tap on my shoulder. I looked up and saw Dave Sabo from Skid Row. I was stunned. I had not spoken to him in at least a year, and I had no idea how he found out about my mother's death. I expressed my shock, and he just hugged me and told how much he respected me and how much I did for him. "Of course I came," he said. I finally broke down. Snake stood with me as I cried.

After the New Year, Charlie Walk and the Promotion Department sent me the largest bouquet of flowers I'd ever seen. I don't know how they knew—I hadn't told anyone in my work life about my mother's death. Somehow, word must have spread, because notes, sympathy cards, phone calls, and fruit baskets came pouring in. Flowers arrived from Joey Demaio of Manowar, as well as Diane Warren, the songwriter I had introduced to Kalodner years before. *How do they know?* I kept thinking. Jason Flom called and offered to take me to lunch. That made me feel good—my onetime best friend still cared. Ahmet sent a huge bouquet and called to say I would always have his support. Even my ex-husband and his new wife sent their condolences. The most touching gesture, however, came from Donnie. He sent flowers and a note signed, "From your Columbia family." It meant everything to me that he would pay his respects and make sure I knew I was part of the team. Like my mother, I thought no one cared about me. These gestures, even from people who had hurt me and whom I had hurt, made me realize just how many friends I had from the music business, how many lives I had touched, and how many people had touched me. It was a healing moment in the midst of terrible grief.

In less than five years, I lost my mother and two of the best men in my life. I had been through a divorce and had lost several jobs. Sometimes it seemed unbearable, like I would never process the pain. I became angry. I felt abandoned by God. I had been questioning my role in the music business for a while, but now I began asking the bigger question: what was my purpose in life? *Signing bands—is that what I'm here for?* I saw the absurdity of the music business compared with the profundity of life and the finality of death. I spent months mourning my mother, and in the process I gained an inner strength and clarity I didn't know I had. I remembered all the ways she had tried to give me a better life than she had, and I knew I had to keep trying to find it. I thought of Tunc, of all people, and the Turkish expression he had: "Dog keep barking, caravan keep moving."

Life goes on. It has no choice.

38

GASLIGHT AND GLITTER

In all my years at Columbia, I never had a relationship with Tommy Mottola. Whenever I saw him in the office, he pretended he didn't know me. That was fine by me—I hadn't forgotten how he buried me with Doug Morris after our first meeting back when I was in A&R at Atlantic. The less contact we had the better.

Tommy was ruthless. No one knew that better than former CBS Records chairman Walter Yetnikoff. Walter had hired Tommy in the late 1980s, not long after Sony bought CBS, and Tommy quickly became Walter's right-hand man. Walter had serious trouble with substance abuse, and by the time Tommy came to work for him, Walter was out of control. At meetings, he'd blurt out things like, "I want David Geffen to teach my girlfriend to give blow jobs," or "Courtney Ross [Steve Ross's wife] has a smelly cunt." Of course, none of this would raise an eyebrow in the music business as long as the money still came rolling in. That's where Walter slipped. He lost $2 billion for Sony, and Tommy began working behind his back to get him fired. It only took two years for Tommy to be named chairman and CEO of the newly named Sony Music.

It didn't take much longer for Tommy to become one of the most hated men in the business. Ahmet always said he was a two-dollar pimp in a $2,000 suit. Tommy thought he was a mobster and would regularly grab his chin and say, "I'm going to see the man." This was code for

Vinny "the Chin" Gigante, head of the Genovese crime family (recall that Tommy was friends with Gigante's brother, and he had courted the Mob since his early days at Buddah Records). He must have believed his own bullshit, because he had the balls to disrespect his own boss, Sir Howard Stringer. He rarely invited Stringer to corporate events. At one Rock & Roll Hall of Fame dinner, he gave Stringer the worst seats in the house. When Stringer called and asked to see him, Mottola's reply was always, "Make an appointment."

Tommy was also extraordinarily competitive and petty. In 1997, Donnie wanted Céline Dion to sing a duet with Barbra Streisand. Tommy insisted it would be bad for Dion, but Donnie pushed ahead with the project. When the song "Tell Him" sold 450,000 copies and became a worldwide hit, Donnie ordered a congratulatory bouquet of 450 roses to be sent to Streisand. Tommy found out about it, called the florist, and ordered 450 roses of his own. He told the florist to send Donnie's flowers the next day.

Like many mobsters—or in this case, wannabe mobsters—Tommy acted paranoid. He regularly pulled up employees' phone records to see who was talking to the media. He kept the blinds drawn in his office, and when guests came, sometimes he'd leave his gun out for display. He hired attorney Michele Anthony to do his job and handle the Japanese corporate owners of Sony. He paid her a fortune to fly to Tokyo and do all the paperwork so he could have his time free to scheme and plot and spy.

He spent much of his day keeping tabs on his wife, Sony's biggest artist, Mariah Carey. Tommy and Mariah married in 1993—he a forty-five-year-old music mogul, she a twenty-three-year-old diva in training. Like many an older man who has snared a beautiful, younger woman, Tommy kept Mariah under lock and key. She couldn't go anywhere without supervision. Tommy dispatched Ann Glew, the wife of Dave Glew at Epic Records, to be Mariah's unofficial House Bunny. When Mariah wanted to ride a roller coaster, Tommy rented out Rye Playland—a huge amusement park in upstate New York—and let the whole company go on a field day. When she wanted to go ice-skating, he rented out the Wollman Rink in Central Park and made all of Columbia

Records skate with her. When she went into the recording studio, no one was allowed to use her name. She was referred to as "Project 50."

Tommy also had Mariah trapped professionally. She was managed by his former partner and doppelganger, Randy Hoffman, of Champion Entertainment. Tommy had owned Champion before taking the job at Sony, and the two men remained close.

By the time I started working for Columbia, cracks had begun to appear in their relationship. In 1996, Mariah Carey was nominated for six Grammy Awards, but she didn't win any (this came after seven nominations and no wins in the previous four years). After the ceremony, Mariah berated Tommy in the lobby of the venue, saying, "What do I need you for? You can't even get me a Grammy." After that, Tommy penned a letter to Mike Greene of NARAS, the recording academy, complaining about the voting rules. Greene ignored his pleas.

What arrogance, to think you could persuade the Grammys to change the rules just because your wife didn't win. And yet, after a decade in the music business, I was no longer surprised by that arrogance. I had grown used to it, and I was tired of it. I was tired especially of how lavishly these men were rewarded for their arrogance—it was rumored that Tommy gave each of his assistants a Mercedes-Benz for Christmas, while he bought a yacht for himself. I used to wonder why the corporate powers would allow such excess, but I came to understand that the music business was just a drop in their bucket. That's how many billions of dollars were involved.

Even after Tommy and Mariah separated in 1997, Tommy still tried to control her. Actor Steven Seagal had a crush on her, and when she was scheduled to perform on *Saturday Night Live*, Seagal contacted the show and asked for tickets. When Tommy found out, he called his old friend Sonny Franzese—the notorious mobster from Buddah Records—and there was no more trouble with Seagal.

Mariah Carey released a video that year for the song "Honey," which portrayed her as a captive in a giant mansion trying to escape a man who was the spitting image of Tommy Mottola (played by *Goodfellas* actor Frank Sivero). She denied that it was supposed to be a commentary on Tommy, but let's just say that many people have found her denial less than convincing. The couple divorced in 1998.

Mariah Carey left Sony for Virgin Records in 2001. This was a huge loss for Sony—she had just won *Billboard*'s Artist of the Decade award, as well as the World Music Award for Best-Selling Female Artist of the Millennium. Tommy gaslit Mariah in the media, and she hired private detective Jack Palladino to investigate him and prove he was the source of planting stories on her. Tommy tried to drive her crazy, and it seemed to work. In the summer of 2001, she began a public and painful breakdown.

Tommy wasn't done with her. As Mariah worked on her first project for Virgin—a movie soundtrack called *Glitter*—he damaged her career in a move that was petty even by music industry standards. Tommy had been secretly watching film rushes from *Glitter*, which contained early versions of the songs Mariah was recording. For one of these songs, "Loverboy," she had sampled the old disco song "Firecracker." She also recorded a slow song featuring a give-and-take vocal with rapper Ja Rule called "If We." Both had hit-single potential.

Tommy approached Irv Gotti—founder of Murder Inc. Records— and asked him for a favor. According to Gotti, Tommy said, "I want you to do this remix for Jennifer Lopez, I want you to put Ja on the record." Before *Glitter*'s release, Jennifer Lopez put out "I'm Real," which used the same sample that Carey had used in "Loverboy." Then, a remix of "I'm Real" came out—it was slowed down and featured a give-and-take vocal between Lopez and Ja Rule in the exact style of Mariah's "If We." The song became a hit, and Mariah couldn't release her songs anymore because Jennifer Lopez had unwittingly stolen them. Carey scrambled to change her songs to differentiate them, but *Glitter* bombed.

In fairness, there were many reasons the film and soundtrack bombed, including a release date of September 11, 2001, but Tommy undoubtedly played a part. Sony still had a stake in *Glitter*, so Tommy wasn't just sabotaging Mariah; he was sabotaging himself. That's how far he would go. Carey said in an interview at the time, "It shouldn't be about finding the new way to mess with me. Like, OK, you've surely done your share of damage. Couldn't we stop now?" Watching this saga unfold, I realized yet again how dangerous the music business was for women. If they'd fuck with the bestselling female artist of the millennium, how could I ever be safe?

39

METEOR

I ENTERED THE 2000S WARILY. Technology was changing faster than ever, and the heads of the music business could not or would not adapt. They were dinosaurs, fighting over the same old turf in the same old ways, while a few of us looked up and thought, *What's that light in the sky?*

In the mid-1990s, music impresario Ricky Adar met with German inventor Karlheinz Brandenburg, the main creator of the MP3. After Adar saw the possibilities of the new technology, he said to Brandenburg, "Do you realize what you've done? You've killed the music industry." He wasn't far off the mark.

The heads of the major labels had good reason to resist the change. The late 1990s had been the most profitable era in music history, driven by the CD boom. CDs cost less than a dollar to produce and sold at roughly seventeen dollars retail. With a profit margin that big, who cared about an arcane technological feat like the MP3?

In 1998, the first consumer-grade MP3 player hit the market. It cost $600 and held five songs—not exactly a threat to the CD. But the MP3 fit the Internet age like a hand in a glove. MP3s shrank huge chunks of data—say, an entire album, or an entire music library—down to a manageable size, and increasing Internet speeds allowed that shrunken data to be shared with ease. It turned out that the light in the sky, the coming doom, was peer-to-peer file sharing. In 1999, the meteor struck: Napster. The age of piracy had begun.

Doug, who by this time was the most powerful music executive in the world, with one-fourth of the entire global market under his control, suddenly became very much against stealing. After all, this was different from selling cleans or cut-outs, or when his company colluded with the other major labels to keep CD prices artificially high, thus in effect stealing half a billion dollars from consumers. This time, someone was stealing from him.

He led the industry's charge to sue the MP3 out of existence, but it wasn't just him. The entire business fought the digital revolution tooth and nail. Eighteen companies joined a lawsuit against Napster. The outcome of the case wasn't important; what was important was that the music business missed the lesson almost completely. The old model was dead. By 2001, the first iPod hit the market. Sony had invented hardware and software for MP3 technology, but they were blind to its power. Steve Jobs beat them to the punch.

Doug had never been a fan of change. When *Billboard* switched to SoundScan technology in 1991, he canceled the subscriptions for Atlantic. SoundScan made sales reporting transparent, and the old guard couldn't continue stealing if there was transparency. However, to Doug's credit, he eventually signed on with Apple after Jobs offered him seventy cents on the dollar for every MP3 sold in the iTunes store. Unfortunately for Doug and everyone else in the business, nothing could stop the coming collapse, which has only gotten worse as digital has replaced physical and streaming has taken over the market.

For me, the digital explosion was just one of many things that sucked the joy out of my job. Life as an A&R executive wasn't as fun as it used to be. In fact, it hadn't been fun for years. I worked for a salary now, not for passion. I spent more time reminiscing about the past than I did dreaming about the future. As I looked back on my career, I realized I had one huge piece of unfinished business: I had to thank Randy Goodman. We hadn't spoken since I was fired, and I had learned and grown so much since leaving RCA—much of it due to Randy's influence—that I wanted to make it right.

Through my contacts in Nashville, I had been keeping tabs on him over the years. In August 1999, I happened to find myself alone with Michael Eisner, then the chairman and CEO of Disney. We spoke about

Lyric Street, which Disney owned, and I told him what a great executive Randy was. I always tried to look out for Randy if the opportunity
presented itself.

I summoned the courage to call him at his office and invite him to
lunch the next time he was in New York City. As fate would have it,
he was coming to New York a few days later with one of his new acts,
Rascal Flatts. His office called back with a date and a place to meet. On
a warm day in September 2000, I walked from my apartment to meet
him at a restaurant across from his hotel. I wondered if he would be
able to see the changes in my face—the loss I had endured, the grief
that occupied my heart. I greeted him warmly with a kiss on the cheek
and sat down. I was nervous. He looked as if the past seven years hadn't
passed. We made small talk. He spoke about his family and what it was
like to be president of a label. It seemed very exciting to me.

Then I got to the point. I thanked him for everything he had done
for me. I told him that he had changed me for the better, that he had
uplifted my spirit each day, given me grace, and provided me with my
first good influence in the music business. He seemed surprised. Then,
in a matter-of-fact tone, he said, "You tried to wear me down, but you
couldn't do it."

I laughed nervously, as though everything were my fault. I didn't
have an explanation for him, and he didn't ask for one. I knew he'd
never understand that he broke me down, too. All I could say was, "I'm
sorry for putting you in an impossible position." We finished our lunch
and said a pleasant good-bye. As I walked away, I couldn't help but turn
around to watch him as he disappeared into the New York City crowd.

I went back to work. Time passed. I spent my days listening to
music and trying to stay out of the gossip and drama. I watched from
the sidelines as piracy ate away at our hits and our profits. Heads began
to roll as revenue cratered. Tommy was fired in January 2003, but as we
have seen, he didn't suffer much. Doug Morris was there to give him
a multimillion-dollar deal at the Universal Music Group. I don't know
what all Tommy did to earn it, but life is good when you have a friend
like Doug Morris.

I didn't miss Tommy. I don't think anyone did—especially not his
former boss. That year at the Sony Grammy party I saw Sir Howard

Stringer standing near the bar. As I approached the bar to get a drink, Sir Howard said, "So this is what I've been paying for all these years." I couldn't help but laugh. Tommy had never invited him to these events.

In April 2003, Donnie left Columbia and was promoted to chairman of the Sony Music Group. I missed Donnie, but I understood that he had to keep moving—he was like a shark. John Ingrassia remained my boss, but I only saw him every couple months or so.

The next few years were unremarkable. In 2006, my contract was due to expire, and I got a call that Columbia wouldn't renew it. I understood. Donnie was gone, and I had no one left to fight for me. I'm not even sure I wanted anyone to fight for me. After twenty years, I said good-bye to my dreams of working A&R and being the vice president of a label. I felt proud to have achieved one of those dreams, but it was time to let the other one go. I had to move on.

40

DOROTHY SEES BEHIND
THE CURTAIN

AHMET'S TOWNHOUSE, NEW YORK CITY, 2006: Ahmet's words hung in the air. After listening to him complain that he hadn't gotten what he wanted out of life, I just turned the question back on him. I asked him why I had never found true love, why my career always seemed to stall, why men passed me over at nearly every job. His answer: "What did you expect? You're a woman."

I didn't know how to respond. I knew it was a bullshit answer, but I still had no rejoinder. In some ways, my time in the music business was more incredible than I could have imagined. In other ways, it had scarred me for life, and Ahmet was one of the men who did the scarring. Two decades after our first meeting in his office, I still felt like his secretary, but I was a different person entirely. I had seen good people die and bad people succeed. I had been harassed, gaslit, abused, and fucked over too many times to count. I never quite reached my dream, but how many people do? How many manage to come as close as I did? Ahmet broke my reverie with a line from his beloved Mick Jagger: "I guess you can't always get what you want," he said. "You get what you need." I wondered if it was really that simple.

Before I left, I told Ahmet I wanted to write about my career, or lack thereof, in the music business. He replied, "Go tell them what

I'm really like. Just wait till I'm dead; I don't want to take all the calls."

Classic Ahmet.

The invitation arrived on a Thursday morning, buried under a pile of catalogs, magazines, and bills. There was no return address, but the back flap was sealed with a gold Atlantic Records logo. I carried it upstairs and opened it at my dining room table. My dog, Pepper—the last remnant of my marriage to Joey Carvello—panted by my feet. The first thing I saw was the name in big black capital letters:

AHMET ERTEGUN
A celebration

It had been four months since Ahmet died. He suffered a brain injury after falling backstage at a Rolling Stones concert. He slipped into a coma, and within a few weeks, he was gone. Eighty-three years old, and he died partying. Leave it to Ahmet.

I scanned the invitation. At the bottom it read, "Invitation is non-transferable." It seemed an odd note to put on an invitation to a memorial, but like everything concerning Ahmet, it was sure to be a hot ticket. The card came loose from the envelope and I tucked it away in my calendar. Of course I would go. Pay my respects. Close a chapter. See old friends—and enemies. It was the end of an era, for music and for me.

Then I noticed the inscription on the inside of the envelope, transposed over a photo of Ahmet: "When you can spend your life doing something you love, you are living a very fine life." I read the line over and over. Ahmet found that kind of love in the music industry. I always hoped I would, but in the end, it was an empty relationship. My definition of a "very fine life" consisted of things I found outside of work, outside of status, even outside of money. My friendships with Charlie, Frank, and Michael meant more than any band I signed; being there for my mother at the end of her life was more important than any hit record I found. I couldn't hang these things on a wall. They weren't gold records, but they carried me like songs.

On April 17, 2007, I went to Lincoln Center for Ahmet's memorial. The auditorium of Rose Hall was filled with a crowd of glitterati from the worlds of music, society, and politics. Bette Midler acted as mistress of ceremonies. Mrs. Ertegun looked somber dressed in black. The Chiquitas sat scattered around the room, along with former assistants, staff members, Atlantic employees, and artists. Doug didn't come.

The ceremony was incredible. Crosby, Stills & Nash sang the Beatles' "In My Life," and Eric Clapton also performed. Even in death, Ahmet could get the Rock & Roll Hall of Fame together. Then the speeches started. When David Geffen took the stage to give his eulogy, I almost laughed. I couldn't imagine anything Ahmet would have hated more. I listened to the other speakers and thought, *If they only knew what Ahmet said about them on a daily basis.* Everyone remembered Ahmet as a mentor, a benign father figure, and an industry legend. The speeches were nice, but they were too . . . *reverent.* Then Mick Jagger spoke. Here was Ahmet's favorite artist, the man he wanted to be more than anyone. Mick looked around the auditorium and said, "Well, I don't know the man these people are speaking of. Ahmet was not like a father to me—more like a wicked uncle." I stood up and applauded. Finally someone had told the truth.

Ahmet was a fucked-up, complicated, brilliant man. He was a historic figure, a legend, and an abuser of substances and people. He gave me my first job and set the tone for the rest of my career. He taught me the most valuable lesson in life: it doesn't matter what others think of you; it only matters what you think of yourself. He also fractured my arm, called me stupid nearly every day, and made unwanted sexual advances at will. What the hell was I supposed to do with that? How was I supposed to make sense of his death, this man who had been both mentor and tormentor, or the death of the magical world he had created at Atlantic Records? Atlantic was truly the House That Ahmet Built, and although the house still stood, something irreplaceable was gone from it forever. I could only thank Ahmet for all he had given and forgive him for all he had done. Dog keep barking, caravan keep moving. It was complex.

It still is.

THE MEN (NOW)

MOST OF THE MEN IN this book still have jobs in the music business.

Doug Morris remained chairman of Sony Music until March 31, 2018. As of this writing, he plans to open his own record company, 12 Tone, to be distributed by Warner Music Group.

Irving Azoff is chairman and CEO of Azoff MSG Entertainment. He is, as far as I know, still a scumbag.

Joe Galante retired from Sony/BMG Music and is now chairman of the Country Music Association Foundation board. He is, by all accounts, still short.

Bob Buziak is retired and enjoying life. I'm happy for him.

Donnie Ienner is a partner in the Lodge, one of the largest ad houses of original music. He is also a board member and partner of Pledge Music, as well as the founder and owner of restaurants Osteria Tulia, Bar Tulia, and the French in Naples, Florida.

Tommy Mottola became a theater producer and is on his third marriage, this time to Mexican recording artist Thalía.

Jason Flom is chairman of Lava Music / Republic Records.

Craig Kallman is cochairman and CEO of Atlantic Records, and still straight as an arrow.

Randy Goodman is chairman and CEO of Sony Music Nashville. He's still McDreamy.

Joey Carvello is still involved in promotion. We remain friendly.

Joel Katz is the undisputed king of music business attorneys.

Ahmet, Charlie, and Frank have all passed away. Frank was the latest to go. He had diabetes and a heart condition, but he didn't give a shit. He didn't take care of himself. In 2011, he had heart surgery and never regained consciousness. I went to see him in a nursing home with Joey DeMaio of Manowar. It was hard to see Frank in that state. I wanted to pull the plug. Frank's cousin came in and slapped him in the face, saying, "Dorothy's here." His eyes opened up. It was like seeing an animal trapped in a body. He died in August 2011.

As for me, after leaving Columbia, I made a lateral move. Having spent so long watching people like Mariah Carey get publicly fucked, I decided to go into crisis public relations. I felt uniquely positioned to help people deal with emergencies like arrest or divorce.

I carry no grudges against any of these men. In fact, they all taught me valuable lessons, even if those lessons often came in shitty ways. I'll leave you with what I learned:

- Don't be a smartass—unless you're already a millionaire, it most likely won't work in your favor.
- Always put the max in your 401K and pension plans—the bastards can fire you, but that doesn't mean you have to be out on your ass.
- Take criticism—don't be defensive; sometimes people are just trying to help.
- If you make a mistake, own it and move on—unless you're very rich, you'll probably have to pay for your mistakes, but if you do it honorably, people will take note of that.
- Be loyal to the paycheck, not the corporation—you don't have to be an asshole about it, but the corporate bosses are rarely your friends.
- Don't gossip—people will hate you.
- Play golf—all the men do.
- Be a team player—don't be petty or jealous of someone else's success.
- Be honest—in a dishonest world, people will notice.
- Deliver bad news immediately—don't, for example, invite someone to a concert the night before you plan on firing her.

- Don't fuck, date, or marry anyone you work with—if you do get involved with a coworker, be prepared for one of you to get fired. If you're a woman, you'll get the short end of that stick.
- Never break the girl code—another woman's husband is just that.
- Stay home from work when you're sick. Coming into the office makes everyone sick.
- Don't confuse your work family with your real family—only one is tied by bonds of blood and love.